Contents

Introduction

Why should kids have to wait until they're older for meaningful service projects?

If you're searching for ways to involve your elementary-aged kids in worthwhile service projects, then look no further. *Hands-On Service Ideas for Children's Ministry* is the book for you!

These hands-on ideas, packed with easy-to-do service projects, will engage, enlighten, and teach kids that to serve others is to serve God.

What happens when you toss a pebble into water? The pebble causes a reaction—the water "rings out." In the same way, your kids' actions will ring out with far-reaching effects!

Each project in *Hands-On Service Ideas for Children's Ministry* is based on one of the "Five Rings of Service"—God, family and friends, church family, community, and world.

Kids will see that God is at the center of every service project—in fact, God is the very reason we serve! And in this book, God stays at the center of service even as kids begin to serve in far-reaching ways.

Not only will your kids learn *who* to serve, they'll learn *how* to serve. Each exciting service idea uses the model of the "Five Styles of Service"—prayer, work, time, money, and donations. Combine the Rings of Service with the Styles of Service, and kids will understand how to serve God and others in ways they won't forget!

To root your kids in the foundations of service, begin by leading them through the fun introductory activities in the first chapter. That way they'll have a firm grasp of how service should be God-centered. Then move on for more ways to serve everyone from the neighbor next door to the neighbor across the globe.

Each service idea in *Hands-On Service Ideas for Children's Ministry* includes a Scripture reference, an easy supply guide, a project prayer, and an extra service step. There's a Scripture index to make it a snap to tie these service ideas into your lesson plans, plus a handy resource index for further inquiries.

So don't make your kids wait any longer! Just turn the page, and start serving!

HANDS-ON SERVICE IDEAS for Children's Ministry

Loveland, Colorado

HANDS-ON SERVICE IDEAS FOR CHILDREN'S MINISTRY

Credits

Contributing Authors: Nancy Wendland Feehrer, Lisa N. Flinn, Nanette Goings, Ken and Susan Kellner, Liz Shockey, and Barbara Younger
Acquisitions Editor: Susan L. Lingo
Editor: Jan Kershner
Senior Editor: Ivy Beckwith
Chief Creative Officer: Joani Schultz
Copy Editor: Janis Sampson
Designer and Art Director: Jean Bruns
Computer Graphic Artist: Randy Kady
Cover Art Director: Jeff A. Storm
Cover Designer: Becky Hawley
Cover Photographer: Jafe Parsons
Illustrator: Kate Flanagan
Production Manager: Peggy Naylor

Library of Congress Cataloging-in-Publication Data
Hands-on service ideas for children's ministry.
p. cm.
Includes indexes.
ISBN 0-7644-2040-2 (alk. paper)
1. Christian education of children. 2. Church work with children.
3. Children—Religious life.
BV1475.2.H336 1998
268'.432—dc21 97-47216
CIP

10 9 8 7 6 5 4 3 2 1 07 06 05 04 03 02 01 00 99 98
Printed in the United States of America.

Serving God—The Reason We Serve

Before leading your class in any of the service projects in this book, first lead them through the introductory service activities in this chapter. These activities will show kids that every service project begins with God. We serve others because we love God and want to follow him. Through these activities, children will understand that when we serve others, we're serving God!

Service Activity #1

WHO DO WE SERVE?

Rings in a Pool of Water

SCRIPTURE *Joshua 24:15; Psalm 100:2 (New Century Version); Matthew 20:26-28; Romans 12:4-6a*

ACTIVITY SUPPLIES ***You'll need*** *Bibles, a round plastic tub, water, and marbles. You may choose to photocopy the Five Rings of Service from page 13 or draw the rings on newsprint or a chalkboard.*

Get Set to Serve

Service starts with God! When we serve others, we're actually serving God. Today you'll demonstrate this concept for your kids by using a simple pool of water.

Before class, photocopy or draw the Five Rings of Service on a large sheet of newsprint or a chalkboard. The Five Rings of Service are God, family and friends, church family, community, and world.

Then set the round plastic tub on a classroom table, and partially fill the tub with water.

The Activity

After children arrive, invite them to sit in a circle on the floor. Ask:

- **What does the word "serve" mean?**

Let kids offer a few ideas. Then say: **The dictionary says that "serve" has more than twenty meanings! The word "serve" can mean to offer food, to help, to spend time, to work, to give honor, and to be obedient. Today we're going to learn about serving.** Ask:

- **Who do you serve in your life?**
- **What do you do to serve others?**

Say: **The Bible says we all have special gifts or talents we**

can use to serve others. Listen to this. Have a child read aloud Romans 12:4-6a. Then ask:

- **What kinds of gifts do you think this passage is talking about?**
- **What kinds of gifts do you see in your family members or friends?**
- **What gifts do you have that you could use to serve others?**

Say: **God has given each of us special gifts to use for him. Now let's find out more about how to use those gifts to serve God.** Invite a child to read aloud Psalm 100:2, then ask:

- **What does this passage say about *how* we should serve God?**

Say: **I think a cheerful person is more pleasant to be around than a grumpy person. Let's do an experiment to see if that's true.**

Ask for two helpers. One will be the Sunny Servant, and one will be the Grumpy Griper. Ask each volunteer to do a simple task such as getting a book from across the room. Have the Grumpy Griper sigh, complain, drag his or her feet, and whine. Next have the Sunny Servant do the same task quickly and cheerfully.

Have kids sit in a circle. Invite kids to vote whether they'd rather associate with a Sunny Servant or a Grumpy Griper. Then say: **Wouldn't it be awful if everyone in our lives were grumpy and unwilling to help? Jesus is a great example of how to be a willing servant of God. He even died on the cross for us! Let's read what Jesus says about serving.**

Invite a volunteer to read aloud Matthew 20:26-28. Then ask:

- **How do you think a king would treat a servant?**

Let kids give examples. Then say: **That's exactly how you would *expect* a king and his servant to act. But in the passage we just read, Jesus says just the opposite. He says that if we want to be first, we must be servants of everyone who needs our help.** Then ask:

- **How can you be a willing servant at home? with your friends?**

Ask a volunteer to read the final passage, Joshua 24:15, aloud. Then ask:

- **How can a person's actions show who he or she serves? Give examples.**
- **What do your actions say about who you serve in your life?**

Say: **When we choose to serve God, we start a chain reaction of events. By serving God, we also serve others. I'll show you what I mean.**

Have kids stand around the tub of water. Pick up a marble and say: **When we serve God, we serve others around us. Let's say**

this marble is a person who has chosen to serve God. Drop the marble in the tub. Say: **See? This one little action affects the whole pool of water. That's just how it is with service. Everything we do as we serve God has an effect on our world.**

Let a few kids take turns dropping the marbles into the center of the water and watching the ripple effect. With older kids you may discuss how the tub is like the world and how even the little things we do can ripple out and affect our whole world.

Show children the Five Rings of Service that you've photocopied or drawn. Point out how the rings of service are similar to the ripples in the tub. Point to each ring of service as you offer the following explanation. Say: **At the center of service is God. Then come the people we're closest to, our family members and friends. Next come our church friends, and finally, our neighbors in the community and our neighbors in the world.**

Hands-On HELP

You might want to use masking tape to make five rings on the classroom floor. Leave the rings in place to remind kids of their service projects and the ripple effect their service has on others.

Activity Prayer

Gather kids together to represent the rings of service. Children can pretend to stand on the five radiating circles of service: God, family and friends, church family, community, and world. (If you have fewer than five kids, have them stand in a regular circle.)

Close with the following prayer. Pray: **Dear God, as we stand in a circle, we know that you are at the center of our lives. Please be with us as we try to be your willing servants. Bless our projects and help us to remember that every time we serve a person in need, we're actually serving you! In Jesus' name, amen.**

Picture This!

SERVICE ACTIVITY #2

HOW DO WE SERVE?

SCRIPTURE

Psalm 100:2 (NCV)

ACTIVITY SUPPLIES

You'll need Bibles, *self-adhesive name tags, markers, old magazines, scissors, tape, paper, and pencils. You'll also need newsprint or a chalkboard and chalk.*

Get Set to Serve

Before class, write headings for the Five Styles of Service on a large sheet of newsprint or a chalkboard. The Five Styles of Service are prayer, work, time, money, and donations.

Also before class, write a character name on each name tag. Suggested names are Dad, Mom, Brother, Sister, Friend, Church Member, Neighbor, and International Friend. If you have more than eight students, add other character names familiar to your kids. For example, you could add Pastor or Choir Leader for the church section or add Police Officer, Librarian, or Grocer for the community section.

To use for the final game, write a service style on a slip of paper for each child in class.

The Activity

As kids arrive, invite them to form pairs, and have partners try to remember *who* we serve. Challenge partners to come up with all Five Rings of Service; then, as a group, have kids call out the rings. Write their answers on the newsprint so that everyone can see.

After you've drawn the Five Rings of Service for the kids to review, distribute Bibles, and have kids read Psalm 100:2 aloud together. Remind kids that we're to serve the Lord with joy!

Next have kids form trios, and give trios paper and pencils. In each trio, have kids brainstorm a list of ways they could serve people in need. Circulate among groups and offer help as needed. Give kids a few minutes to brainstorm, then ask trios to share their ideas.

Hands-On HELP

The Five Rings of Service are God, family and friends, church family, community, and world. Consider drawing the rings on poster board to keep as a colorful classroom display.

Write kids' suggestions on a separate sheet of newsprint.

Next ask kids to be very specific. For example, if kids suggested giving something to the needy, ask them exactly what they would give. Write those suggestions on the newsprint as well.

When kids have finished brainstorming, show kids the Five Styles of Service you wrote on newsprint before class. Explain that each of their suggestions can fit into one of the Five Styles of Service.

Categorize kids' ideas into the five service styles by writing a letter code next to each idea: "P" (prayer), "W" (work), "T" (time), "M" (money), and "D" (donations). You might want to use a different-colored marker for each service style.

Next have kids go through magazines and cut out pictures that show examples of each of these service styles. (You may want to save these pictures to put on your bulletin board in the third service activity.) Tape these pictures with each service-style heading.

To reinforce the ideas of *who* we serve and *how* we serve, try this next activity with your kids. Have them stand in a line facing you. Give each child one of the self-adhesive name tags you prepared before class. One at a time starting with "Dad," have each student tell one positive thing to do for the character on his or her left. Play the game two or three times. Then add an extra challenge!

Hand each person a slip of paper with one of the styles of service written on it. Have children each say a way they could serve the person next to them using that service style.

Challenge kids to remember and use these styles of service every day!

Activity Prayer

Gather kids together, and thank them for their cheerful participation in class! Then join with kids in a circle, and offer the following prayer: **Dear God, you've blessed this group with so many talents, interests, and abilities! Please help us remember that by serving you with joy, we can serve the people in our families, our church, our neighborhoods, and the world. Help us to remember Jesus' humble example every day so that by giving our prayer, work, time, money, and donations, we can serve you and inspire others to do the same. In Jesus' name, amen.**

Putting It All Together

SERVICE ACTIVITY #3

CREATING A BULLETIN BOARD

SCRIPTURE

Psalm 100:2 (NCV); Proverbs 4:7

ACTIVITY SUPPLIES

You'll need *a Bible, a bulletin board, paper, a stapler, paper letters, markers, tape, clean scissors, paper plates, fruit leather, and photocopies of the "Say It With Service!" bulletin board idea from page 13.*

Get Set to Serve

During the next class session or two, you and your kids will be designing and putting together a "Say It With Service!" bulletin board. The bulletin board will be used to illustrate to church members what your kids are learning about service and will include the elements of "Who We Serve" and "How We Serve." You may also want to use the bulletin board to highlight some of the terrific service projects that you're working on as the year progresses.

Before class, set out the paper, stapler, letters, scissors, tape, and markers. You may also want to use the magazine cutouts from the "How Do We Serve?" activity.

Hands-On HELP

Let your congregation in on the fun by displaying your bulletin board in a highly visible spot in your church.

The Activity

As kids arrive, review the material covered in the first two service activities. Have kids form pairs, and challenge them to remember who we serve (God, family and friends, church family, community, and world); and how we serve (by utilizing prayer, work, time, money, and donations). Be sure to let pairs work together and give each other hints so everyone is a winner!

Then have kids repeat or read together Psalm 100:2 (NCV). Say: **Let's remember in all we do to serve God with joy!**

Invite a child to read aloud Proverbs 4:7 for the rest of the class. Then say: **Now that you've become wise about who we serve and how we serve, it's time to share that wisdom with others. Together we're going to create a bulletin board for all the people at church.**

Give kids each a copy of the "Say It With Service!" handout (p. 13).

The handout will help kids as they brainstorm ideas to create a bulletin board that is uniquely their own.

After kids agree on the overall design and details, have them form the following super-server groups. The "letter-getters" can either hand-draw letters, cut out letters from magazines, or punch out perforated letters. The "cut-ups" can cut the paper and design the pictures for the board. And the "cling-ons" can staple or tape the letters and pictures to the board.

When the board is completed, have kids make a simple presentation to the congregation indicating where to look for the bulletin board and what it is trying to convey. Each child can explain one of the Rings of Service or one of the Styles of Service. (If you have more than ten kids, let several children give examples of ways to serve in each category.) Don't be surprised if people come up later and say, "I never thought of service like that before!"

Kids may want to celebrate what they've learned about service by making edible "service snacks." Using paper plates, have kids write a ring of service or a style of service at the top of each plate. Be sure they prepare enough plates so there's one for each child.

Shuffle the prepared paper plates, then turn them face down on a table. Have kids each choose a plate. Then give each child a piece of fruit leather and a pair of clean scissors. Ask each child to cut an edible fruit-leather example of the ring of service or the style of service written on the plate. For example, if the style of service is money, a child could cut a pretend dollar bill from the fruit leather.

When kids have finished cutting, let each child present and explain his or her handiwork. Then let kids gobble up their super-server snacks!

Activity Prayer

Gather kids together in a circle, and offer the following prayer: **Dear God, thank you for letting us serve you. Help our bulletin board be a reminder that you want us to share what we have. Inspire those who look at it to serve in ways they hadn't thought of before, and please bless their efforts. Help us to be generous with our time and our possessions, to be faithful in serving you, to be sensitive to others' needs, and to serve you with joy! In Jesus' name, amen.**

Bulletin Board

Serving Family and Friends

In this chapter, kids will enter the next ring of service, serving family and friends. Use the following service projects to help children see that they can serve God by helping, encouraging, and praying for their family members and friends.

Kids will get to know their neighbors with this yummy service project.

Neighborly Cakes

RING OF SERVICE

- ☑ God
- ☑ Family/Friends
- ☐ Church Family
- ☐ Community
- ☐ World

STYLE OF SERVICE

- ☐ Prayer
- ☐ Work
- ☑ Time
- ☐ Money
- ☑ Donations

SCRIPTURE

Proverbs 3:27-29

Service Supplies

You'll need a Bible, small slips of paper, a small container, pencils, quart-sized resealable plastic bags, flour, sugar, baking soda, pumpkin pie spice, and measuring cups and spoons. You'll also need photocopies of the "Neighborly Cake" recipe from page 18.

Hands-On HELP

You may wish to include the story of the Good Samaritan found in Luke 10 as further background for this service project.

Get Set to Serve

Gather kids together. Have a child read aloud Proverbs 3:27-29. Then ask:

- **What makes a good neighbor?**
- **Why does God want us to be good neighbors?**

Then say: **The Bible has many stories about being kind to each other and being good neighbors. Jesus tells us that everyone is our neighbor and we should be kind to all people. Let's play a game of Neighborly Charades to see how much we really know about our neighbors.**

Give each child a slip of paper and a pencil. Have kids write activities that they've seen their neighbors doing, such as mowing the lawn, washing windows, working on a car, getting the newspaper, unlocking the door, or pulling weeds. Put all the paper slips together in a container.

Then let each child take out a slip of paper. Tell kids that on the count of three they are all to act out the activities on their papers. Have kids guess what others are acting out. If a child knows what another child is doing, have him or her shout out the action. If correct, the child whose action was guessed may stop and sit down for a rest. Continue until all of the neighborly actions have been guessed.

The Project

Say: **Just as we learned in our game, neighbors do many things. We can also be kind and neighborly to them in many ways.** Have kids brainstorm ways to be neighborly. They might suggest shoveling the snow from neighbors' sidewalks or visiting neighbors when they see them outside. Say: **We can also give them a special neighborly treat. Let's make some yummy cake mixes that we can give to our neighbors, who will in turn make some more to give to another neighbor, and so on throughout the whole neighborhood!**

Have kids form an assembly line to make cake mixes. Each child will add an ingredient to each bag of cake mix. If you have a large group, have kids work in pairs or trios. You'll need two bags of cake mix for each child to take home. Each quart-sized resealable bag will need to have

1 ½ cups flour,
1 cup sugar,
1 teaspoon baking soda,
2 teaspoons pumpkin pie spice, and
1 copy of the recipe.

Seal up the bags. Have each child take home two bags of cake mix. One bag is to use with his or her family, and one bag is to be passed on to a friend or neighbor with instructions for the neighbor to make a cake and pass a cake mix on to someone else.

Hands-On HELP

Consider baking and bringing one of the cakes for your class to enjoy. The kids will love knowing how their own cakes will taste.

Project Prayer

Thank the children for being such good neighbors and serving others by giving away their cake mixes. Invite the kids to hold hands, and ask each child to pray for a neighbor by name. If children don't know the name of a neighbor, encourage them to just say "my neighbor" when it's their turn to pray. Close the prayer by thanking God for the good neighbors in your class. End with a group "amen."

The Extra Service Step

As a class, take church brochures, monthly newsletters, or advertising flyers about an upcoming event along with your cake mixes to the neighborhood surrounding your church. For safety's sake, go as one large group, always sticking together.

Neighborly Cake

Pour your cake mix into an ungreased 9" square pan. Make three "holes" in the mixture in the pan. Pour 4 tablespoons vegetable oil into the first hole, 1 tablespoon white vinegar into the second hole, and 1 teaspoon vanilla into the third hole. Then pour 1 cup cold water over all the ingredients, and stir well. Bake at 350 degrees for 35 minutes.

Now be neighborly, and make a cake mix to pass on to another neighbor. The mix contains the following ingredients: 1½ cups flour, 1 cup sugar, 1 teaspoon baking soda, 2 teaspoons pumpkin pie spice. Be sure to include one copy of this "Neighborly Cake" recipe.

Neighborly Cake

Pour your cake mix into an ungreased 9" square pan. Make three "holes" in the mixture in the pan. Pour 4 tablespoons vegetable oil into the first hole, 1 tablespoon white vinegar into the second hole, and 1 teaspoon vanilla into the third hole. Then pour 1 cup cold water over all the ingredients, and stir well. Bake at 350 degrees for 35 minutes.

Now be neighborly, and make a cake mix to pass on to another neighbor. The mix contains the following ingredients: 1½ cups flour, 1 cup sugar, 1 teaspoon baking soda, 2 teaspoons pumpkin pie spice. Be sure to include one copy of this "Neighborly Cake" recipe.

Prayer Pillows

RING OF SERVICE

- ☑ God
- ☑ Family/Friends
- ☐ Church Family
- ☐ Community
- ☐ World

STYLE OF SERVICE

- ☑ Prayer
- ☐ Work
- ☐ Time
- ☐ Money
- ☐ Donations

SCRIPTURE

Ephesians 6:18

Service Supplies

You'll need a Bible, scissors, old magazines and newspapers, tape, fabric markers, and photocopies of the "Pillowcase, Please!" handout from page 21.

Get Set to Serve

One week or more prior to the "Prayer Pillows" activity, send home a copy of the "Pillowcase, Please!" handout with each child.

On the day of the project, have kids form groups of three. Give each group scissors and a few magazines and newspaper sections. Ask groups to cut out pictures of family members doing things together. They might find pictures of moms and kids, brothers and sisters, or grandparents. After each group has cut out several pictures, have kids tape the pictures to a wall. Gather kids in a circle near the pictures and ask:

- **What are these families doing?**
- **What kinds of things do you like to do with your family?**

Say: **It's fun to do things with people in our families. It's also fun to do things *for* the people in our families.** Ask:

- **What kinds of things do you do for the people in your family?**

Say: **In the Bible, Paul tells us about something very important that we can do for others.** Have a child read aloud Ephesians 6:18. Then ask:

- **What does this verse say we can do for our families?**
- **What kinds of things can we pray about for our families?**
- **When is a time God answered your prayers for your family?**
- **How is prayer a way to serve our families?**

Say: **This verse says to pray "on all occasions." We can talk to God whenever we want to, any time of the day or night! It's also good to set up regular times every day to talk to God.** Ask:

- **What time of day do you like to talk to God?**

Say: **A lot of people like to pray at bedtime, when they can talk to God about what happened during the day and pray about what might happen tomorrow. We're going to make prayer pillows to remind us to pray every night for the people in our families.**

The Project

Have several extra pillowcases on hand in case you have a visitor or a child forgets to bring one in. You can find inexpensive linens at a thrift shop or garage sale.

Set out the pillowcases and fabric markers. The children will each draw pictures of the people in their families or extended families on the pillowcase. Suggest that kids draw pictures about family vacations they've enjoyed, favorite activities the family enjoys together, or places family members spend lots of time, such as work and school.

As children work, talk informally with kids about their families. Explain that these pictures can remind kids that God is always watching over their families, no matter where they are. Tell kids they'll be taking their pillowcases home to remind them to pray every night for their families.

Project Prayer

Have the children lay their pillowcases side by side in a big circle. Then have kids spread out and lie on the floor with their heads on their pillowcases. Have kids close their eyes and pray silently for their families. End with a group prayer, thanking God for giving us families.

The Extra Service Step

Using an extra pillowcase, have kids draw self-portraits or write their names on the pillowcase. Include your name and the names of some of your church leaders as well. Each week send the pillowcase home with a different child so he or she can pray for each person named on the case. Make sure kids know to wash the pillowcase before bringing it back to class.

Pillowcase, Please!

Our group will be learning about serving our families through prayer. We're going to make special "prayer pillowcases," and we need your help. Please bring one white or light-colored pillowcase. (A used pillowcase will be fine.) Please bring the pillowcase in by________________________________.

Thank you!

Pillowcase, Please!

Our group will be learning about serving our families through prayer. We're going to make special "prayer pillowcases," and we need your help. Please bring one white or light-colored pillowcase. (A used pillowcase will be fine.) Please bring the pillowcase in by________________________________.

Thank you!

Permission to photocopy this handout from *Hands-On Service Ideas for Children's Ministry* granted for local church use. Copyright © Group Publishing, Inc., P.O. Box 481, Loveland, CO 80539.

Kids will make and send encouraging postcards to parents at work.

RING OF SERVICE

- ☑ God
- ☑ Family/Friends
- ❑ Church Family
- ❑ Community
- ❑ World

STYLE OF SERVICE

- ☑ Prayer
- ❑ Work
- ☑ Time
- ❑ Money
- ❑ Donations

SCRIPTURES

1 Thessalonians 5:11

Positive Postcards

Service Supplies

You'll need a Bible, local phone books, plain postcards, pens, markers, stamps, and cheerful stickers.

Get Set to Serve

Gather children together and ask:

- **What types of jobs do your parents have?**
- **What are some of the hard things about their jobs?**

Say: **Your parents may feel tired and discouraged after a long, hard day at work. You may know what that feels like from your own experience with hard days at school.** Ask:

- **When have you had a hard day at school? What happened?**
- **How do you feel when you have a day like that?**
- **What makes you feel better when you're having a bad day?**

Say: **Sometimes a few kind words go a long way toward making a bad day better. I'm sure your parents would love to be cheered up and encouraged during the middle of a difficult day. The Bible says in Thessalonians that we should encourage one another. Listen.** Have a child read aloud 1 Thessalonians 5:11. Then say: **Let's do a fun service project to encourage our parents at work!**

The Project

Using local phone books, children will look up their parents' workplaces and copy the full addresses, including ZIP codes, onto postcards. You could also ask parents for their work addresses when they drop their kids off or send home a request form the week before.

For various reasons, some kids may prefer to use their

home addresses rather than work addresses, which is fine. After kids have addressed the postcards, discuss the following questions with them. Ask:

- **What are some words or phrases people use to encourage each other?**
- **How could you decorate the card to cheer up your hard-working parents?**

Have children use markers to decorate the postcards and write encouraging words or phrases on the cards. Suggest using phrases such as "Thanks for your hard work!" "I'm thinking of you!" or "I hope your day is super good!" Colorful stickers such as stars, smiley faces, hearts, and rainbows will make the cards extra-cheerful. Add stamps to the cards if they don't come with postage paid. Gather up the cards, and mail them that day.

Then ask a child to read the verse from Thessalonians again. Ask:

- **Do you think these cards will encourage your parents at work? Explain.**
- **How would you feel if you received a card like this during a hard day at school?**
- **What are some other ways we can encourage our friends and family members this week?**

Project Prayer

Say: **Encouraging one another is like giving each other a pat on the back. Let's gather in a circle with each of us facing the back of the next person. We'll pray around the circle with encouraging pats on the back. I'll start the "encouragement" prayer.** Pat the child in front of you on the back and say: **Thank you, God, for bringing** (name) **to our class.** (As the prayer continues around the circle, remind kids that this is a time for prayer and affirmation, not a time to see who can hit the hardest.)

The Extra Service Step

Have kids think about other people in their lives who might need encouragement, such as friends, grandparents, uncles and aunts, teachers, and pastors. Kids can send these people additional postcards.

Family members will benefit from this helpful gift of time.

RING OF SERVICE

- ☑ God
- ☑ Family/Friends
- ❑ Church Family
- ❑ Community
- ❑ World

STYLE OF SERVICE

- ❑ Prayer
- ❑ Work
- ☑ Time
- ❑ Money
- ❑ Donations

SCRIPTURE

Colossians 3:23

Choose-a-Chore

Service Supplies

You'll need a Bible, tape, a spray bottle of all-purpose cleaner, paper towels, staplers, scissors, markers, a cassette player, and a cassette of favorite upbeat praise music. Also, for each child, you'll need one chenille wire, two paper plates, and a photocopy of the "Helping Hands" handout from page 27.

Get Set to Serve

Gather kids together in a room which gets plenty of use, such as your fellowship hall. Ask:

- **What kinds of activities take place in this room?**
- **What are some of the most fun events you remember here?**
- **Have these activities ever been a little messy? Explain.**

Say: **Any room that people use a lot is bound to get messy or dirty. And everyone who uses a room needs to help keep it clean. Most of us have used this room at one time or another, so now let's give a few minutes of our time to clean it!**

Set out the spray bottle of cleaner and the paper towels. Spray a little cleaner on a paper towel for each child, and instruct kids to wipe table tops, chairs, doorknobs, and other washable surfaces. As kids are working, play a cassette of their favorite praise music.

Hands-On HELP

If time allows, feel free to expand this activity by suggesting ways for kids to pick up and tidy the room. Kids might clean out the supply closet, empty trash cans, and even clean the floor! Be sure to check with your custodian or sexton first.

The Project

While kids are working, set out the "Helping Hands" handouts (p. 27), staplers, scissors, and markers. After kids have been cleaning for five or ten minutes, turn off the cassette tape, and gather kids in a circle near your supply table.

Say: **Thank you! You all did such a great job of cleaning! Just look at how much better the room looks. Thanks for taking the time to help.** Ask:

• **Does your family like to save or keep things? Does saving things ever create a problem? Explain.**

• **Does your house ever get messy?**

Say: **Let's take turns naming one activity we do at home that makes a mess. I'll start: One messy activity we do at our house is...**

Give an example of something you do at home that makes a mess. For example, you might say, "washing the dog," "cleaning the fish tank," or "making peanut butter sandwiches." Then go around the circle, giving each child a chance to add an example of a messy activity.

Say: **We may not always like the idea of taking time to clean up our messes. Doing chores may not seem like such fun work. Listen to what the Bible says about the work we do.** Have a child read aloud Colossians 3:23. **Whatever we do, even if it's a chore we may not enjoy, we can do it as service to God. That's especially true at home.** Give each child a "Helping Hands" handout. Say: **This handout shows lots of ways to help at home.** Ask:

• **Which chores on this handout are your favorite to do? Which don't you like?**

• **Which chores take the most time? Which are the easiest?**

Let kids use markers to color and decorate their handouts. Then give each child one chenille wire and two paper plates. Ask kids to each write "My Gift of Time" on the back of one of their plates. On the back of the other plate, have each child draw the numbers of a clock face.

Then have kids each cut their chenille wires in half and cover one end of each half with tape. (If you have very young children, do this and the next step yourself before class.) Show kids how to use scissors to carefully punch a hole in the center of the clock face.

Demonstrate how to insert the taped ends of the chenille wire pieces through the hole in the plate and how to twist the ends of the wires together. When kids turn their plates over, they'll have movable clock hands!

As kids work, praise them for how much cleaning they accomplished earlier in such a short amount of time. Discuss household jobs that can be done in five or ten minutes, such as making a bed or sweeping the kitchen floor.

When kids have completed their clock faces, show them how to staple the two plates together around the edges, leaving an opening at the top large enough for a hand to reach inside.

Hands-On HELP

If you have non-writers in your class, you can quickly write, "My Gift of Time" in pencil for children to trace with markers. You might also want to draw a sample clock face on the chalkboard for young children to copy.

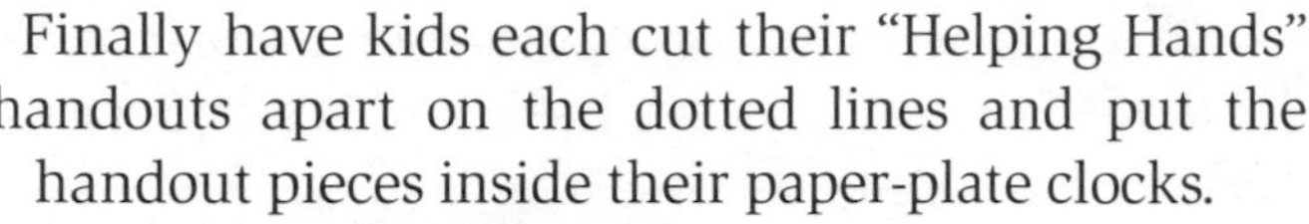

Finally have kids each cut their "Helping Hands" handouts apart on the dotted lines and put the handout pieces inside their paper-plate clocks.

When children have finished, say: **These paper-plate clocks can represent your gift of time to your family. Take these clocks home and give them to your parents. Then each day this week, reach in and choose a chore to do at home. Your family will appreciate your help, and you'll know you're really doing something to help, just as you did here today!**

For fun, set your clock hands to the amount of time you think the chore you've chosen will take. For example, if you think the chore will take ten minutes, set the clock for ten minutes after twelve. Then when you've completed the chore, see how long the job actually took!

Project Prayer

Invite kids to stand in a circle, holding the clocks in their hands. Pray: **Dear God, the hands of a clock tell the time, but the hands of these kids will bring a helpful gift of time. Please bless these children and their families today and always. In Jesus' name, amen.**

The Extra Service Step

Have each child make a second "gift-of-time" clock to be given to a grandparent or neighbor. When the child visits that person, he or she can offer "helping hands."

Another idea is to give kids a blank paper, and ask them to draw pictures showing special chores that need to be done at their homes, such as cleaning the guinea pig's cage or filling the bird feeder. On the top of their pictures, have kids write, "I promise to..." and at the bottom of the pictures they can sign their names. Each bonus chore can be presented to a parent, brother, or sister.

Helping Hands

Sweep	Wash	Sort
Empty	Pick Up	Dust
Put Away	Feed	Make Bed

Fluffy

Using ordinary loaves of bread, children will create "loving loaves" with a special message to share with family and friends!

Loving Loaves

RING OF SERVICE

- ☑ God
- ☑ Family/Friends
- ❑ Church Family
- ❑ Community
- ❑ World

STYLE OF SERVICE

- ❑ Prayer
- ❑ Work
- ❑ Time
- ❑ Money
- ☑ Donations

SCRIPTURE

Matthew 4:4;
John 6:35

Service Supplies

You'll need Bibles, construction paper, glue sticks, markers or crayons, scissors, ribbon, a hole punch, cups of water, and a variety of breads. (Bread samples may include Greek pitas, Mexican tortillas, French croissants, Italian grissini, German pumpernickel, and Jewish challah.) You'll also need photocopies of the "Request for Bread" handout from page 31 and the "Loving Loaf" handout on page 32.

Get Set to Serve

A week prior to the "Loving Loaves" lesson, photocopy the "Request for Bread" handout, and send a copy home with each child. Each student will need to bring one loaf of bread to the next class session. Any kind of bread will work as long as it is in a plastic, not paper, bag. (Specialty breads will make the project special to the kids.)

On the day of the lesson, you may want to provide extra loaves in case someone forgets or you have visitors in your class. You'll also need to bring in several types of bread for the children to sample.

Before class, cut sheets of construction paper in half horizontally. You'll need a half sheet for each child. Also, cut a twelve-inch length of ribbon for each child.

As children arrive, have them set their bread on a table. Invite them to look at the variety of breads that were brought. Then have kids sit in a circle on the floor. Ask:

- **What do people need to stay alive?** (Answers might include food, water, air, shelter, and clothes.)

Say: **People all over the world need the same things to stay alive. Food is one of the most important things that we need to live. And bread is one food that people all over the world eat. We're going to try some of the breads that are favorites around the world.**

Hold up each type of bread, tell children its name, and what country it originated from. Pass around samples of the different breads you brought. You also may want to provide water or juice for kids to drink between samples.

After kids enjoy the bread samples, invite two children to read Matthew 4:4 and John 6:35 aloud for the rest of the class. Then ask:

● **Jesus tells us that bread is important, but what else do we need to live?**

● **Who is the Bread of Life? Why do you think Jesus calls himself that?**

Say: **Bread is very important, but Jesus says that we also need to believe in him to live. He says that we can't live on bread alone, but on every word that God tells us. Today we're not only going to share bread, but we're going to share the good news of Jesus, too!**

The Project

Set out markers or crayons, construction paper, glue sticks, photocopies of the "Loving Loaf" handout (p. 32), a hole punch, ribbon lengths, and scissors.

Explain that each child will make a card to attach to a loaf of bread. Then each child will give a loaf of bread to a friend or family member who needs to hear about Jesus or be reminded of his love.

Let each child choose a loaf of bread and a half sheet of construction paper. Have kids fold their sheets of paper in half to form cards. Then give each child a photocopy of the "Loving Loaf" handout. Have kids cut out the bread slices from their handouts. Kids will glue the top slice of bread to the front of their cards and the other bread slice inside their cards. Encourage kids to decorate their cards with crayons or markers. Be sure to have kids sign the inside of their cards.

If there are extra loaves of bread, kids who finish their cards early may help make extra cards. When cards are complete, give each child a length of ribbon. Have kids each punch a hole in the upper left corner of their cards, and thread a length of ribbon through the hole. Kids can use this ribbon to attach the cards to the loaves.

As kids are working, encourage them to be thinking who they can give their loaves to.

Project Prayer

When the cards are attached to the loaves, gather kids together in a prayer circle. Explain that you're going to say a responsive prayer of thanksgiving to God. Say that you'll say a sentence and then the kids will respond by saying, "Thank you, God!" Tell kids that at the end of the prayer you'll all say "amen" together. Lead kids in the following prayer.

Teacher: Dear Father, you've given so much to us! To you we say...
Kids: Thank you, God!
Teacher: For our families and friends, we say...
Kids: Thank you, God!
Teacher: For giving us our daily bread and all we need to live, we say...
Kids: Thank you, God!
Teacher: For the gift of your Son Jesus, we say...
Kids: Thank you, God!
Teacher: For the ability to give to others and share the good news about Jesus, we say...
Kids: Thank you, God!
Teacher: Dear God, you've given so much to us! Give each of us one more thing—a grateful heart.
All: Amen!

As kids leave, encourage them to take their Loving Loaves and give them away as soon as possible. Tell kids they'll have a chance next week to describe how their service projects were received. (Be sure to remember to ask kids about their experiences next week!)

The Extra Service Step

Get involved in providing "bread" world-wide! Write or call these organizations to see what kids can do to help.

• Bread for the World (Christians united against poverty and hunger.)
1100 Wayne Avenue, Ste. 1000
Silver Spring, MD 20910
(301) 608-2400

• National Committee for World Food Day (Projects that kids can be involved in.)
2175 K St. N.W.
Washington, DC 20437
(202) 653-2404

Next week we'll be doing a service project called **"Loving Loaves."** We'll share our bread and our faith with families and friends. Please bring to class one loaf of bread in a plastic bag.

We'll also be sampling bread varieties from around the world. See you then!

Thanks!

Next week we'll be doing a service project called **"Loving Loaves."** We'll share our bread and our faith with families and friends. Please bring to class one loaf of bread in a plastic bag.

We'll also be sampling bread varieties from around the world. See you then!

Thanks!

Loving Loaf

This bread is given to you
by someone who thinks you're special!

Dear ________________________________,

I wanted to share this bread and message with you because I think you're special—to me and to God!

Then Jesus declared, "I am the bread of life.
He who comes to me will never go hungry,
and he who believes in me will never be thirsty
(John 6:35)."

Enjoy!

Love,

____

Kids will collect prayer and praise requests from family and friends to learn about and share the power of prayer!

Prayer Power Packs

RING OF SERVICE

- ☑ God
- ☑ Family/Friends
- ☐ Church Family
- ☐ Community
- ☐ World

STYLE OF SERVICE

- ☑ Prayer
- ☐ Work
- ☐ Time
- ☐ Money
- ☐ Donations

SCRIPTURE

Philippians 4:6; 1 Thessalonians 5:16-18; James 5:13,16b

Service Supplies

You'll need Bibles, colored file folders, paper, a stapler, scissors, small envelopes, glue sticks, crayons or markers. You'll also need photocopies of the "Prayer Request Form" handout from page 37 and the "Prayer Request Instructions" handout from page 36.

Get Set to Serve

A week before this project, photocopy the "Prayer Request Form" handout (p. 37) and the "Prayer Request Instructions" handout (p. 36). Give each child four copies of the prayer form and one copy of the instructions. Briefly go over the instructions with the children, and answer any questions they may have. Be sure they understand the assignment.

Before class, prepare a file folder notebook for each child by stapling ten to twelve sheets of paper inside each file folder. You may want to make a few extra notebooks in case you have visitors.

Gather children together in a circle. Ask:

- **What is prayer?**
- **When do you pray?**

Say: **The Bible talks a lot about prayer. Let's take a look at some of those passages right now.** Have kids form trios, and give each trio a Bible. Have kids take turns in their trios reading Philippians 4:6 and 1 Thessalonians 5:16-18. Then have a volunteer in each group read the passages aloud.

Have kids discuss the following questions within their trios. After each question, ask for a few volunteers to share their groups' insights with the rest of the class.

Ask:

- **When does the Bible say we should pray? When do you pray?**
- **When is it hard for you to pray?**
- **Why should we pray?**

After discussions, have trios come together into a circle. Then have another child read James 5:13 aloud for the class. Say: **Wow! It looks as though we should always be in communication with God!** Ask:

- **Do you think there's ever a time that prayer wouldn't be a good idea? Why or why not?**
- **Do you think there's anything you couldn't pray to God about? Explain.**

Say: **Praying is like having a direct telephone line to God! Let's read on a little further in that last Bible passage to see just how powerful prayer can be.** Have another child read aloud James 5:16b. Then say: **This passage says that prayer can be powerful and effective. Think of a time recently when God answered one of your prayers. Turn to a partner and describe what happened.** Give kids a few moments to share their experiences. If you have time, let a few children describe their answered prayers for the class.

Then say: **Now think of a family member or friend who could use prayer right now. Don't say the person's name, but keep that person in mind as we do our service project today.**

When we think of serving other people, we often forget that prayer is one of the best and most powerful ways to serve! We just read about how powerful prayer can be. Now let's put that power to work by making Prayer Power Packs!

The Project

Before class, each child will have interviewed four family members or friends and collected their prayer requests on the forms you handed out last week. Have kids cut apart the prayer requests. The prayer requests will be put in the Prayer Power Packs. Kids will use the packs to help keep track of prayer requests and God's answers to prayer.

Set out envelopes, glue sticks, and crayons or markers. Give each child a file folder notebook that you prepared earlier. Show the children how to glue one envelope to the inside front cover of the notebook and one envelope to the inside back cover. Have kids put the prayer requests in the front envelope. The back envelope will be for answered prayers.

Invite each child to decorate the cover and print "Prayer Power

Pack" on the front of the notebook. Older kids may also want to write one of the Bible passages read earlier on the cover.

Say: **Now I'm going to teach you one way to pray that will help you remember to pray for others.** Show kids how to draw two intersecting lines, one vertical and one horizontal, on the first page of their notebook to divide the paper into four squares. With older kids, you may want to make an analogy to the cross with these intersecting lines. You can also read aloud Hebrews 2:18 about Jesus knowing what it is like to suffer in this world and being wonderfully able to help us.

Thanks!	I'm sorry
Help me to...	Please be with...

Have kids write, "Thanks!" in the upper left square. Have them write, "I'm sorry" in the upper right square. In the lower left square, have them write, "Help me to..." And in the last square, have kids write, "Please be with..."

Invite kids to fill in each square with their current prayer needs. Remind them to look in their envelopes and to include these requests in the last square. (Younger kids can draw pictures of their prayers, and older kids can use words.) This is a quick and easy way to teach kids how to pray.

Say: **Each day you can divide a new prayer page into the same four sections. This will help you keep track of your own prayers and help you to serve God by serving others with prayer!**

When you see God answer a prayer, write a note about it, and put the note inside the rear envelope. You'll soon have an envelope full of answered prayers! Keep your Prayer Power Pack handy to remind you to pray and to remind you of God's faithfulness in answering prayer.

Project Prayer

Gather kids together. Thank them for their time and attention in learning that prayer can be a powerful tool for serving others.

Before your closing prayer, challenge kids to listen to your prayer carefully and see if they can hear the four prayer parts: "Thanks!" "I'm sorry," "Help me to..." and "Please be with..."

Hands-On HELP

Assure members of the congregation that prayer requests will remain confidential within your class. Then make sure that kids understand and abide by that confidentiality. You may want to suggest that especially sensitive requests be anonymous.

Then pray a prayer similar to the following one.

Dear Father,

***Thank you* for the power of prayer!**

***We're sorry* that we don't pray as often as we should.**

***Help us to* remember to turn to you when we're in need and when we're joyful.**

***Please be with* these kids as they use their Prayer Power Packs to experience first-hand your magnificent power!**

In Jesus' name, amen.

The Extra Service Step

Try extending your prayer service project to the whole church. Hand out copies of the "Prayer Request Form" with the bulletins at your worship service. Members of the congregation can deposit the prayer requests in the offering plate or in some other designated spot.

Read the requests with your class each week, and ask volunteers to pray aloud for the people involved. Encourage people to report how God answers their prayers. Have your kids make a class Prayer Power Pack to keep track of the requests and answered prayers.

Prayer Request Instructions

Next week, we'll be doing a service project for our family and friends! We'll be creating Prayer Power Packs to keep track of our prayers and to remind us to serve others by praying for them.

Please ask four friends or family members to share their prayer needs. Ask them to fill out a "Prayer Request Form." Be sure to bring these forms with you next week.

Prayer Request
Name:
Prayer Need:

Prayer Request
Name:
Prayer Need:

Prayer Request Form

Please share your special needs with us by filling in the prayer requests below. We will cut the requests apart and track God's answers by using our Prayer Power Packs that we make in class. **Thank you!**

Prayer Request

Name: ______________________________

Prayer Need: ______________________________

____

____

Prayer Request

Name: ______________________________

Prayer Need: ______________________________

____

____

Prayer Request Form

Please share your special needs with us by filling in the prayer requests below. We will cut the requests apart and track God's answers by using our Prayer Power Packs that we make in class. **Thank you!**

Prayer Request

Name: ______________________________

Prayer Need: ______________________________

____

____

Prayer Request

Name: ______________________________

Prayer Need: ______________________________

____

____

Help kids find the fun in being a servant with this project.

RING OF SERVICE

- ☑ God
- ☑ Family/Friends
- ☐ Church Family
- ☐ Community
- ☐ World

STYLE OF SERVICE

- ☐ Prayer
- ☑ Work
- ☐ Time
- ☐ Money
- ☐ Donations

SCRIPTURE

Ephesians 6:7-8

Trusty Dusters

Service Supplies

You'll need Bibles, a chalkboard and chalk or newsprint, a permanent marker, baby powder, and a trash can. You'll also need scissors and one old bath towel for every four children. You could also use old washcloths, providing one for each child.

Get Set to Serve

Using the permanent marker, draw lines on the towels, dividing each towel into four equal sections.

Before this lesson, prepare a "dusting area" in a separate room or a special corner of your room. Set up one or more tables, depending on the size of your class. Four children will stand at each end of a table. Cover the tables with baby powder. Make sure children are kept away from the powdery tables until the designated time.

Have children sit in a circle on the floor and ask:

- **Does anyone know what a servant is?**

Allow children time to respond, then say: **A servant is someone who helps others. We all want to learn to serve God, so that makes us his servants. But we can't see God, so we can't give him a glass of water or a hug. How can we serve him if we can't see him? Let's read a verse from Ephesians that will help us know what he wants us to do to serve him.** Have a child read aloud Ephesians 6:7-8. Then ask:

- **How are we supposed to serve? Why?**
- **Has anyone been a servant today? What did you do?**

Say: **There are lots of ways to serve others. Let's think of as many different ways to serve others as we can.**

Write children's responses on the newsprint. Children may suggest things they do at home to help their parents or kind ways they act toward friends at school or church.

Then say: **Now we're going to make Trusty Dusters to help you serve, and then we'll play a game with our Trusty Dusters.**

The Project

Set out scissors and bath towels or washcloths. (If washcloths are used, children won't need to cut them.) Show children how to start a cut in the towel on one of the marked lines. Then encourage kids to help each other tear off the sections. You may want to pair younger children with older helpers as they use scissors.

As children work on the tear-off towels, talk about how the towels will help them serve. Explain that they're making Trusty Dusters, a tool they'll be able to use at home, school, or church. Ask children to give examples of ways to use the towels to serve others.

Kids might suggest that at school they could use the Trusty Dusters to help clean chalkboards. In their homes, they could dust the furniture. Remind children that when we serve others, we're actually serving God.

Once children have their towels torn and in hand, have them follow you to the prepared tables. Encourage children to form groups of four around each end of the powdery tables.

Before the activity, young children will enjoy singing the following song from Ephesians 6:7-8 to the tune of "Frères Jacques."

Do your work,
Do your work
Happ-i-ly,
Happ-i-ly.
Work as if you are
Ser-ving the Lord.
Serve the Lord.
Serve the Lord.

Challenge older kids to draw pictures in the powder of themselves acting out various acts of serving others. Let kids take turns guessing what each other's pictures portray.

After kids sing or draw for a few moments, say: **Now you'll all get a chance to practice your dusting abilities! When I say "go," everyone should start dusting until the tables are clean.**

Once children have cleaned the tables (and the "dust" has settled!), let kids shake out the extra powder in the towels over a trash can.

Hands-On HELP

If your dusting area is carpeted, use the baby powder sparingly, or substitute confetti that can be easily vacuumed up.

Hands-On HELP

Rather than dusting, consider having kids clean the chalkboard or classroom windows with their Trusty Dusters.

Project Prayer

Have kids come together in a prayer circle. Thank children for helping to clean the tables and for learning more about being servants. Invite kids to each hold the edges of a neighbor's towel to form a circle. Ask volunteers to pray a special promise to use their towels to serve others. After the prayer, have children lift the towels up and join in saying, "Amen!"

Encourage kids to take their Trusty Dusters home and find as many ways to use them to serve others as they can this week. Say that next week, kids can compare notes on how they used the towels.

The Extra Service Step

Turn kids loose in the sanctuary with their Trusty Dusters, and watch the dust fly! (Check with your church sexton first.) Make sure to mention to the adults that the children spent time cleaning the sanctuary. It will help reinforce children's joyful and willing service if someone recognizes the children's efforts and thanks them. During the following week's lesson, ask the children how their parents responded to the "Trusty Dusters" service project.

Kids will put together kits so they can serve their families by washing the family cars.

Carwash Kits

RING OF SERVICE

- ☑ God
- ☑ Family/Friends
- ☐ Church Family
- ☐ Community
- ☐ World

STYLE OF SERVICE

- ☐ Prayer
- ☐ Work
- ☑ Time
- ☐ Money
- ☐ Donations

SCRIPTURE

John 13:3-5, 12-15

Service Supplies

You'll need Bibles, several big sponges that can be cut up, scissors, old towels or cloth that can be cut or torn into rags, measuring cups, plastic resealable bags, detergent, paper sacks, markers, a stapler, and a few photocopies of the "Car Stencil" from page 43. For each child, you'll need photocopies of the "Carwash Instructions" handout from page 44.

Get Set to Serve

Before class, set up four project stations around your room. At the first station, set out large sponges and scissors. At the second station, set out scissors and old towels or cloth. At the third station, set out measuring cups, plastic resealable bags, and powdered laundry detergent. At the fourth station, set out paper grocery sacks, colored markers, and car stencils.

Gather kids together in a circle on the floor. Ask:

- **After a hard day at work, what do you think your parents' feet feel like?**
- **What would you say if they asked you to get a bowl of warm water, some soap, and a towel to wash their feet?**

Say: **In the Bible, it says that Jesus served his disciples by washing their feet.** Ask children to take turns reading aloud John 13:3-5 and 12-15. Then say: **In Bible times, people wore sandals all day long on dusty, dirty streets.** Ask:

- **What do you think it would be like to wash their feet?**
- **How was washing their feet an act of service?**
- **Why does it seem surprising that Jesus would be serving his disciples that way?**

Say: **By washing his disciples' feet, Jesus gave us a powerful example of serving others. If Jesus, God's Son, served others, we should serve others, too. Sometimes it may seem hard to**

serve others. We're used to being served. Our parents have been serving us since we were tiny babies. Ask:

- **What are some ways our parents serve us?**
- **What are some ways we can serve our parents?**

Say: **Today we're going to create kits that will help you to serve your parents. We're going to put together some tools so you'll be able to wash your family's cars or other vehicles.**

The Project

Each child will make a Carwash Kit, complete with four tools to use to wash the family cars.

Have kids form four groups: the Steady Spongers, the Ready Rippers, the Super Soapers, and the Special Sackers. At each station that you have set up, kids will make components for the Carwash Kits. You'll need a kit for each child in class.

At the first station, the Steady Spongers will cut up the sponges into smaller pieces. At the second station, the Ready Rippers will use scissors to make beginning cuts in the towels or cloth, then rip them into smaller pieces. At the third station, the Super Soapers will each pour one-third cup of the detergent into plastic resealable bags. At the fourth station, the Special Sackers will decorate the paper sacks using markers and car stencils and write, "Carwash Kit" on each one.

After kids finish preparing the kit components at their stations, have them each assemble a Carwash Kit by putting the components into a decorated sack. Then give each child a copy of the "Carwash Instructions" to staple to the sack. As children work, suggest other ways to use the kits, such as cleaning barbecue grills or patio furniture.

Project Prayer

Have kids sit in a circle. Say: **We can also serve our parents by praying for them.** Allow volunteers to pray for their parents. Then close by praying for all parents and asking God to help kids serve.

The Extra Service Step

Organize a carwash on a Saturday morning at your church. Kids can put announcements in the church bulletin and hang posters up around the community. They can bring buckets, sponges, and towels from home. Let children set out a "donation tub" for their chosen cause—perhaps a missionary in a country where clean water is scarce. Choose a volunteer to make sure that all proceeds go toward the cause.

Car Stencil

Photocopy this car stencil pattern onto thick paper, and cut it out to use for decorating the Carwash Kit bags.

Carwash Instructions

1. Gather supplies: Carwash Kit, bucket, hose, and bathing suit, if it's hot!

2. Hose down the car. Make sure the windows are **up!**

3. Put detergent into bucket, and fill with water.

4. Dip the sponge into the bucket, and scrub the car.

5. Hose down the car again.

6. Dry the car with the towel.

7. Pick up any trash from inside the car, and put it into the paper bag.

Serving Our Church Family

In this ring of service—serving their church family—children will begin to understand that Christians are all part of God's family. The service projects in this chapter will help kids see how they can serve these "family members," too—the members of their own church family!

Kids will pull weeds and feed their faces in this fun service project.

Weed 'n' Feed Party

RING OF SERVICE

- ☑ God
- ☐ Family/Friends
- ☑ Church Family
- ☐ Community
- ☐ World

STYLE OF SERVICE

- ☐ Prayer
- ☐ Work
- ☑ Time
- ☐ Money
- ☐ Donations

SCRIPTURE

Matthew 13:24-30, 36-39

Hands-On HELP

Be sure to make a master list of what's needed, and make reminder calls a few days before the party to help kids remember to bring their ingredient for the Weed 'n' Feed Salad. You may need to supply the ingredients for those kids who aren't sure they will be able to come.

Service Supplies

You'll need Bibles, plastic grocery bags or lawn-and-leaf bags, a clump of grass, and a large weed. You'll also need photocopies of the "Weed 'n' Feed Party" handout from page 48.

Get Set to Serve

A week before the project, photocopy and send home with the kids the "Weed 'n' Feed Party" handout. Make sure to circle a food item for each child to bring. If you have more than six kids in your class, assign more than one child to bring lettuce, cheese, and beef. You'll also need to supply paper plates, plastic ware, paper cups, a dessert, and drinks. (If you have enough kids bringing food items, assign these items, too.)

On the day of the project, pull up a clump of grass and a large weed before class. As children arrive at church or at your designated area, place their food items in a refrigerator or in coolers. Gather the children together and hold up the grass and weed. Ask:

- **Where do weeds come from?**
- **What makes this plant something we want to keep in our yard and this weed something we want to pull out?**
- **Who decides what is a weed and what is a plant?**

Then say: **Weeds are even mentioned in the Bible.** Ask a volunteer to read aloud Matthew 13:24-30. Ask:

- **What do the wheat and weeds represent in this parable?**
- **Why do you think Jesus told this parable?**

Continue with the parable by asking another volunteer to read Matthew 13:36-39. Then ask:

- **What is this parable really about?**
- **Who or what are some "weeds" in our lives?**

Kids might say that friends sometimes ask them to do wrong things, that they're tempted to cheat on a test, or that they want to take something that belongs to someone else.

Say: **Jesus wants us to be productive wheat—strong Christians—even though we may be surrounded by weeds!**

The Project

Say: **Let's pull some weeds out of our lives to become more productive wheat.** Give each group of two or three kids a plastic grocery bag. Have kids go out on the church property and pull weeds or go to a nearby park with an adult and pick up trash. Check with your church or community staff to see where kids can be of most use. Have extra bags on hand for kids who fill their bags. You can even make this a little more fun by setting a time limit to collect the most trash or weeds.

Make sure that kids stay within safe boundaries and have plenty of adult supervision.

Have kids return to the church, wash up, and create their own Weed 'n' Feed Salads. Set up an assembly line of the ingredients. Let each child select how much of each ingredient he or she wants. Or have kids crush the chips and mix all of the ingredients together to create one big salad. Before eating, pray together the project prayer below.

Project Prayer

Have kids create a fun prayer cheer with one group calling out the words to "Jesus Loves Me" and the other group repeating the words. End with a rousing group "amen!"

The Extra Service Step

Have your group "own" an area of the church property by keeping it maintained. How about planting some flowers in one of the flower beds? A weekly addition to your Sunday school or club time together could be to water and spiff up your area.

Weed 'n' Feed Party

Please join us for a Weed 'n' Feed Party at ____________________ (location)

on ________________ (date) at ____________________ (time). Come in your grubbies, ready to Weed 'n' Feed. Please help us with the "Feed" portion of the party by providing the following circled item:

1 pound of shredded lettuce
$^1/_2$ pound of grated cheddar cheese
1 pound of cooked ground beef
3 diced tomatoes
1 16-ounce jar of salsa
1 bag of tortilla chips

Weed 'n' Feed Party

Please join us for a Weed 'n' Feed Party at ____________________ (location)

on ________________ (date) at ____________________ (time). Come in your grubbies, ready to Weed 'n' Feed. Please help us with the "Feed" portion of the party by providing the following circled item:

1 pound of shredded lettuce
$^1/_2$ pound of grated cheddar cheese
1 pound of cooked ground beef
3 diced tomatoes
1 16-ounce jar of salsa
1 bag of tortilla chips

Permission to photocopy this invitation from *Hands-On Service Ideas for Children's Ministry* granted for local church use.
Copyright © Group Publishing, Inc., P.O. Box 481, Loveland, CO 80539.

These prescriptions are guaranteed good medicine for anyone!

Peppy Prescriptions

RING OF SERVICE

- ☑ God
- ❑ Family/Friends
- ☑ Church Family
- ❑ Community
- ❑ World

STYLE OF SERVICE

- ❑ Prayer
- ❑ Work
- ☑ Time
- ❑ Money
- ❑ Donations

SCRIPTURE

Acts 20:35

Service Supplies

You'll need Bibles, white paper, plenty of index cards, markers, pens, tape, and stickers. Also collect large circular containers with lids, such as oatmeal containers or coffee cans with the edges taped.

Get Set to Serve

Before class, clean the containers. Also cut the index cards in half.

Say: **Sometimes when people get sick they don't get well right away. Sometimes they even have to stay in the hospital for a long time. Sickness makes people weak, and it takes time to get strong again.** Ask:

- **Have any of you ever been in the hospital? What was it like?**
- **Has anyone ever had to stay home sick from school before? Why?**
- **What did you do all day when you were home?**

Let children talk about their own experiences of staying home or being in the hospital. Then have a child read aloud Acts 20:35. Ask:

- **What does it mean that it's more blessed to give than to receive?**
- **How do you feel when you help someone or give someone a gift?**

Then say: **All of us have had times when we've been sick and felt bored at home or in the hospital. It would have been nice to have had something special to do, wouldn't it? Well, did you know that there are members of our church who are sick right now? I know that they would love to have something special to do.**

The Project

Set out all the supplies on a work table in the room. Explain that each child can make several notes or pictures of encouragement to go into the containers. The containers will be given to church members who are ill.

Encourage younger children to draw colorful pictures and write their names on the backs. Older children may want to write short notes or copy Scripture verses onto the cards. Show children how to fold the cards and place them into the prepared oatmeal containers. Have kids work together to make large labels out of white paper. Have volunteers write, "Peppy Prescriptions" on the labels, and then ask other children to tape them over the real labels of the containers.

While children are working on their notes and drawings, discuss others in the church who might need encouragement. Let children suggest other ways to reach out to members of the congregation.

Project Prayer

Have children sit in a circle. Thank them for their willingness to serve by sharing their time and love with people in the church. Close by having kids repeat each phrase of the following prayer:

Lord Jesus (repeat),
Help us to work as Paul did to help the weak. (Repeat.)
Help us remember your words (repeat)
"It is more blessed to give than to receive." (Repeat.)
Amen. (Repeat.)

The Extra Service Step

Keep supplies on hand, and ask the church secretary or pastor to let the group know when congregational members are hospitalized. Sharing "peppy prescriptions" can become a great ongoing ministry that would tie the children to the rest of the church.

Kids will learn the importance of God's Word through this fun service project.

Bible Basics

Service Supplies

You'll need Bibles, a dictionary, forty to fifty pieces of tagboard or thick paper, stickers, markers, glue, crayons, a hole punch, and colored yarn.

Get Set to Serve

Before class, cut the tagboard into 3x8½-inch strips. Also cut colored yarn into five-inch lengths.

Have kids join you in a circle, sitting on the floor. Set a dictionary in the middle of the circle, and encourage kids to look through it. Ask:

- **Who decides what the names of items should be? How do we know that a chair is a chair?**
- **Who decides what words are in the dictionary?**
- **How would the world be different if there were no dictionaries?**

Kids might answer that publishers and scholars decide what words go in dictionaries and that we would all have different definitions of words without dictionaries. Distribute Bibles to kids, and have them read 1 Peter 1:24-25 aloud together. Then ask:

- **What is the Bible?**
- **Who decided what stories and poems were put in the Bible?**
- **How would the world be different if the Bible had never been written?**

Then say: **The Bible is very different from dictionaries. People write dictionaries, but the Bible comes from God. The Bible is God's Word. Let's play a fun game to learn a little more about the Bible.**

Designate one wall in your classroom to be the "Yes" wall and one wall to be the "No" wall. Make sure to clear all of the furniture out of the middle of the room. Have kids stand in the middle of the room.

RING OF SERVICE

- ☑ God
- ☐ Family/Friends
- ☑ Church Family
- ☐ Community
- ☐ World

STYLE OF SERVICE

- ☐ Prayer
- ☐ Work
- ☑ Time
- ☐ Money
- ☐ Donations

SCRIPTURE

1 Peter 1:24-25

Hands-On HELP

You can choose to modify the movement back and forth between walls to galloping, crawling, crab-walking, or rolling.

Hands-On HELP

This game can be adapted for older kids by having them form groups and find specific Bible references to create and answer questions. They will need Bibles with concordances.

Then say: **When I ask one of the following yes-or-no questions about the Bible, hop to the wall with the best answer for you. Remember, you may not always need to go along with the crowd—there may be some questions that will have different answers for each person.**

Use the following yes-or-no questions or make up your own.

- **The Bible is the Word of God.** (Yes)
- **I read the Bible every day.** (Yes/No)
- **By the time you're a grown-up, you should have read the whole Bible.** (Yes/No)
- **The Bible has a story in it about a man who eats locusts with honey.** (Yes)
- **If you wanted to sing a song, you could find the words to many songs in the book of Psalms.** (Yes)
- **You always have to read the Bible before you go to bed.** (Yes/No)
- **There is a woman named Priscilla in the Bible.** (Yes)
- **People need to read the Bible.** (Yes)

Then say: **The Bible is God's Word. When we read the Bible, we get to know God better. The Bible is known to be the Book of Books. It has stories, poems, songs, and history in it. Just think, reading the Bible is like reading hundreds of different books at the same time!**

Let's serve the people in our church by making Bible bookmarks for the Bibles in the sanctuary. That way, we'll all be able to find just the right story in the Bible when we read the Bibles during church.

The Project

Set out the tagboard strips, yarn, hole punch, and miscellaneous art supplies. Then let creativity rule! Show kids how to punch a hole in the end of each bookmark, loop several lengths of yarn through the hole, then tie the yarn in a knot as a decorative tassel.

Let each child decorate numerous bookmarks. When the kids are finished decorating, lead them into the worship area. Let them place the completed Bible bookmarks in the pew Bibles to be used by the congregation each week. Be sure to include a note in your worship bulletin next week telling about the bookmarks and the service project. The kids may also wish to each take one Bible bookmark home to use in their own Bibles.

Project Prayer

While kids are still in the sanctuary, thank them for serving the church in this important way. Have them open a pew Bible and read together the prayer-song written in Psalm 29:1-2. Close by leading the group in a corporate "amen." Encourage kids to mark this Psalm with their new Bible bookmarks so others will open right to it next week.

The Extra Service Step

Take this project one step further by working with church leadership to include kids in your class as lectors or readers in the church service. Try to continue this service on an ongoing basis, such as once a month.

Make up a treasure hunt for your church leaders to follow and find encouraging "treasures."

Pastor Treasure Hunt

RING OF SERVICE

- ☑ God
- ☐ Family/Friends
- ☑ Church Family
- ☐ Community
- ☐ World

STYLE OF SERVICE

- ☐ Prayer
- ☐ Work
- ☑ Time
- ☐ Money
- ☐ Donations

SCRIPTURE

Hebrews 13:7

Hands-On HELP

You may want to include other church leaders in this fun project. Consider treating office staff, children's and youth ministry workers, music directors, and custodians to a treasure hunt, too!

Service Supplies

You'll need treats and other little gifts that your pastors might enjoy, such as cookies, candy, balloons, books, and so on. You'll also need newsprint, markers, paper, pencils, tissue paper, tape, and ribbon.

Get Set to Serve

Gather kids together in a circle on the floor. Tape a sheet of newsprint to a wall. Say: **Let's list some of the things our pastors have to do during a typical week.** Help kids brainstorm some of the many duties a pastor has. Ideas might include preaching, studying the Bible, praying, counseling, visiting the sick, performing marriages and funerals, figuring out the budget, coordinating the staff, and so on.

After writing the list, say: **Wow, what a list! How do pastors find time for their families, friends, or even for themselves? Pastors have a very special job. They also have a very hard job.**

Pastors show us how to serve others in the church. They spend time teaching us from the Bible, talking to people who need help with their problems, and visiting sick people in the hospital. Ask:

- **When was a time a pastor served your family or someone you know?**

You may want to tell about a time a pastor helped you or your family. Then ask:

- **What do people do to show they appreciate their pastors?**
- **What are some ways we could say thank you to our pastor?**

Say: **Pastors help us a lot, and they do it because they love God. They teach us about God and serve as our spiritual leaders.**

The Bible talks about leaders in Hebrews 13:7. Have a child read aloud Hebrews 13:7.

Say: **The Bible tells us to remember our leaders, and one way to do that is to show them we care about them. Let's do a fun service project to remember our pastors every day this coming week and encourage them with our gifts.**

The Project

Set out the little gifts you brought to encourage the pastor, such as cookies, candy, balloons, books, and so on. You might also want to have kids make pictures and cards to hide instead of the gifts or to accompany the gifts. The number of gifts depends on how many days you want to do the treasure hunt, how many pastors serve your church, and how many kids you have in your class.

Have kids wrap the gifts in tissue paper and ribbon. Then let them hide the gifts in different locations around the church. As kids work on the gifts, discuss how the pastoral leaders have served the church and how these gifts are a way of giving service to the pastors. Ask:

- **How do you feel when somebody notices your hard work or your special talents?**
- **How will these gifts make our church leaders feel?**
- **How are we serving our church leaders by doing this project?**

Have kids make a treasure map guiding the pastor(s) to the gifts they have hidden. Ask a volunteer to write, "Thank you, Pastor (name), for serving us!" Then have kids roll up the map and tie it with a ribbon. If children hide gifts for each day of the week, have them make a map for each day and write the day of the week on it. If kids hide different gifts for different pastors, ask them to write the pastors' names on the outside of the maps.

Have the class present the map to the pastor and explain the project. The pastor will definitely feel remembered and will probably get a chuckle from the kids' encouragement.

Hands-On HELP

Encourage church leaders who receive the "treasured" gifts to thank the kids in person or with a handwritten note.

Project Prayer

After the gifts have been hidden and the maps made, call the kids together. Tell children that God will be happy that they "remembered their leaders" by giving them gifts of thanks. List the pastors' names and ask for volunteers to pray for each of them, thanking God for their examples of serving.

The Extra Service Step

Let the pastors see who is thanking them by making "Instant Picture Thank You Cards." Bring in an instant-print camera, and take pictures of each child involved in the Pastor Treasure Hunt.

Have kids each make a construction paper card and glue the picture on the front. Let kids decorate their cards and write a big "Thank You, Pastor" on the front. Have the kids each write a note telling why they're thankful for the pastor, and make sure kids sign their cards. Send the cards to the pastor when the Pastor Treasure Hunt is over.

Kids will decorate and sell shoelaces to support a project at church, encouraging one and all to wear the "gospel of peace."

Snazzy Shoelaces

RING OF SERVICE

- ☑ God
- ☐ Family/Friends
- ☑ Church Family
- ☐ Community
- ☐ World

STYLE OF SERVICE

- ☐ Prayer
- ☐ Work
- ☐ Time
- ☑ Money
- ☐ Donations

SCRIPTURE

Ephesians 6:15

Service Supplies

You'll need a Bible, packs of new white shoelaces in both children's and adult sizes, and fabric pens or permanent markers in a variety of colors. You'll also need a sticker for each child. Blank index cards and a hole punch are optional.

Get Set to Serve

To ensure success in this project, use the following guidelines. Be sure kids use fabric pens or permanent markers to decorate the shoelaces, otherwise the decorations may run if the laces get wet.

Make samples of the shoelaces to show the kids. Dots, stripes, and blocks of color work well.

To keep the laces from becoming tangled and to display them in an eye-catching manner, you may want to punch holes in index cards and thread the laces through the holes. Consider writing part of the Scripture verse or simply "Ephesians 6:15" on the display cards, or having the kids do this after the laces are decorated.

Let kids decide how to go about selling the shoelaces. They can sell them from a table for several weeks after church or create posters advertising the laces and then take orders. Set a selling price for the laces that you think is appropriate for your congregation.

Then let the kids decide how the money raised from the sale will be used. They might consider contributing to a local charity or sending the money to missionaries.

As a project warm-up activity, kids will each be given a sticker to put on their shoe. Try to find stickers with a Christian theme

Hands-On HELP

If you don't want to sell the shoelaces in church, consider setting up a plan with your kids to give the shoelaces away to needy children. Kids could then donate money of their own or ask friends and family for donations. Or kids could sell the shoelaces to family members or friends to raise money for the project (with parental approval, of course).

such as a cross or dove or with a Scripture verse on them. If you can't find these, foil stars (also a Christian symbol) are easy to locate in most stores that sell stationery or office supplies.

When kids arrive, begin with the warm-up activity. Ask them to sit in a circle, preferably on the floor.

Begin by having a child read aloud Ephesians 6:15. Then ask:

- **What does it mean to have "your feet fitted with the readiness that comes from the gospel of peace"?**
- **How can we as Christians stand strong?**
- **How can we show God's love and peace to other people?**

Then say: **To stand strong as Christians means to make our faith the most important part of our lives. Jesus teaches us to love one another. As Christians, it's our job to let the world see our love and to show others what our faith means to us.** Ask:

- **When are times it's hard for you to be peaceful?**
- **How can you live out the gospel of peace this coming week?**

If kids have trouble thinking of ways to show peace, offer suggestions such as

- writing a letter to an elderly relative,
- inviting someone who seems unhappy at school to sit with them at lunch or on the bus,
- telling a friend about their church and its activities, and
- taking a few moments to speak to a neighbor.

When everyone in the circle has had a turn to talk, tell how you plan to live out the gospel of peace in the coming week. Then say: **I'm going to give you each a sticker to wear on your shoe today. The sticker will help you remember to live out the gospel of peace this week.** You may want to briefly explain the symbol or words on the stickers. Make sure to put a sticker on your shoe, too!

The Project

Hands-On HELP

You may want to have your kids wear decorated laces, in shoes or as necklaces, when they're promoting this project or selling the laces.

Next explain the Snazzy Shoelace Sale. Show the sample shoelaces, give kids decorating suggestions, and let them decide how they will go about selling the laces. Finally, help them decide what the money will be used for at your church.

Say: **When we raise money with our Snazzy Shoelace Sale, we'll be showing Christian love by donating the money to a good cause. We'll be living out the gospel of peace by helping others. All those who purchase and wear our shoelaces will be fitted with the gospel of peace, too, because they're helping support a good cause.**

Have kids decorate the laces, and be certain to admire their work. When the laces are decorated, have children thread them onto display cards if they have decided to do so.

Carry out the plan for selling the laces, keeping kids in the forefront of the project as much as possible. Make sure your congregation understands what the money will be used for and include the Scripture verse in any publicity.

Project Prayer

As a closing prayer, lead kids in a march around the room. Pray: **Dear God, help us to wear the gospel of peace on our feet.** Ask kids to fold their hands but keep their eyes open as they march. Repeat the sentence prayer three or four times, then conclude: **We pray in the name of Jesus. Amen.**

The Extra Service Step

Consider holding this fund-raising project around the time when a walk-a-thon is taking place in your community. Encourage participants to purchase laces to wear in their shoes for the event. If folks don't have shoes that take laces, the laces can be worn as colorful necklaces, bracelets, or placard holders on the day of the walk.

Kids team up with seniors to brighten the lives of sick or shut-in church members, families with new babies, or hurting families.

Bright Bulbs!

RING OF SERVICE

- ☑ God
- ☐ Family/Friends
- ☑ Church Family
- ☐ Community
- ☐ World

STYLE OF SERVICE

- ☐ Prayer
- ☐ Work
- ☑ Time
- ☐ Money
- ☑ Donations

SCRIPTURE

Matthew 25:34-40; Romans 12:13

Service Supplies

You'll need a Bible, empty two-liter bottles, dirt, fast-blooming flower bulbs, water, index cards, construction paper, double-sided carpet tape, craft sticks, scissors, crayons or markers, plastic bowls, and photocopies of the "How to Care for Your Bright Bulbs" handout on page 63.

Get Set to Serve

Before the service project, contact seniors in your church who would like to participate in this project with the kids. They can lend their gardening expertise and their experience in serving others! Let them know the time and place your group will be meeting.

Also find out from the pastor or the church office who in the congregation could use a little cheering up. Make a list of these people and their addresses. You may also need to call them in advance to arrange a time to drop off their Bright Bulb Pots.

On separate cards, write the name of each person and why they need cheering up (if appropriate). These will be given to your kids so they can make cards to accompany the Bright Bulb Pots.

Wash the two-liter bottles, and peel off the labels. Then cut each bottle so that about six inches remains. You'll need one "bottle bottom" for each child in class.

As children and seniors arrive, ask them to form intergenerational pairs and sit together at your work table. If you don't have enough senior visitors to form pairs, have kids form small groups, making sure there's a senior in each group. As you wait for everyone to arrive, encourage pairs to "interview" each other about hobbies and interests.

When everyone has arrived, offer a brief word of welcome and thank the seniors for being a part of this important service project. Have seniors and kids discuss the following questions in their pairs,

Hands-On HELP

For a special touch, have kids make and send invitations to the seniors who will be joining you for the project.

then ask volunteers to share insights from their discussions with the rest of the group. Ask:

- **When are times you need cheering up?**
- **What are some ways others try to cheer you up?**
- **Have you ever missed a fun activity because you were sick at home? What was that like?**
- **What makes you feel better when you're sick in bed?**
- **How is cheering others a way of serving God?**

Say: **Listen to this story that Jesus tells in the Bible.** Ask a senior and his or her partner to take turns reading aloud Matthew 25:34-40. Then ask:

- **What are some ways this passage says we can help others?**
- **According to this passage, who are we really serving when we help others?**

Say: **That's right. When we serve others, we're really serving God because that's what he wants us to do.**

Ask another senior and his or her partner to read aloud Romans 12:13. Before they read, explain that this verse was written by the Apostle Paul, who was talking about Christians and how they should behave toward one another. Ask:

- **What needs do you think fellow Christians might have?**
- **What needs do you think people in this church might have?**

Say: **Jesus tells us that we should visit and help those who are in need. The Bible also says that we should love other Christians and help with their needs. Today we're going to make Bright Bulb Pots to cheer up some church friends who could use a bright spot in their lives!**

The Project

Set out scissors, construction paper, craft sticks, carpet tape, and the prepared two-liter bottle "pots." Show kids and seniors how to cut out construction paper flowers to attach to the pots with carpet tape. Invite them to work together with their partners to cover the whole pot with bright, cheerful flowers.

Set up a separate table (or a station outside if the weather is nice) with dirt and bulbs. Have kids and seniors fill the pots halfway with dirt. Then have partners each place a bulb in the center of the pot and cover it with more dirt. Let partners water the bulbs sparingly.

When the flower pots are complete, pairs will each make a simple card with instructions on how to care for the bulbs. They'll also write a cheerful message to accompany the gift.

Give each team a card with the name of a church member who needs a little cheering up. Show pairs how to cut out the "How to Care for Your Bright Bulbs" instructions (p. 63) and glue the instructions on a half-sheet of construction paper. On the back of their papers, encourage pairs to write messages of cheer to their church friends in need. Have them attach the cards to the craft sticks.

If at all possible, try to arrange for the seniors and their partners to deliver the Bright Bulb Pots together. If this can't be done, take pictures of the church members receiving their gifts. The children will be thrilled to see how they can serve others with such a simple, yet meaningful, act of kindness!

Project Prayer

Have children and their senior partners hold hands in a circle. Thank them for working so well together for the benefit of people who need their help. Then offer this prayer:

Dear God, you are the hope of the sick, the joy of the sad, the comfort of the weary, and the light for those still in darkness. Help these bulbs brighten many lives and remind our special friends that you care for every living thing—most especially your beloved children in need. In Jesus' name, amen.

The Extra Service Step

Reach out to the community with God's love! Bake loaves of quick dill herb bread. Tuck a seed packet of dill into a small clay pot to accompany the bread. After the bread is enjoyed, the pot can be filled with dirt and the seeds can be planted. Attach a nice card with instructions and a message filled with hope! Donate these to a local food bank to be given to families, compliments of your church!

How to Care for Your

Bright Bulbs

- Keep your Bright Bulb Pot in a warm, sunny spot.
- Keep the soil moist, but not soggy.
- Keep watching your pot for a beautiful creation of God!

How to Care for Your

Bright Bulbs

- Keep your Bright Bulb Pot in a warm, sunny spot.
- Keep the soil moist, but not soggy.
- Keep watching your pot for a beautiful creation of God!

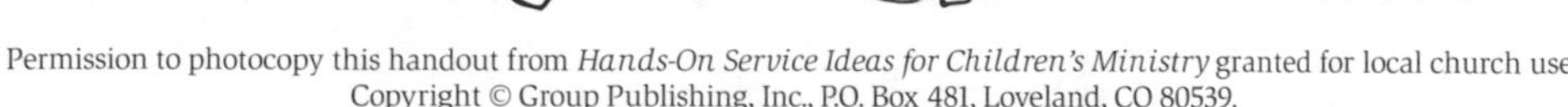

Permission to photocopy this handout from *Hands-On Service Ideas for Children's Ministry* granted for local church use.
Copyright © Group Publishing, Inc., P.O. Box 481, Loveland, CO 80539.

Kids will practice being good stewards of the earth and of your church by cleaning up the church building and its grounds.

Terrifically Tidy

RING OF SERVICE

- [x] God
- [ ] Family/Friends
- [x] Church Family
- [ ] Community
- [ ] World

STYLE OF SERVICE

- [ ] Prayer
- [x] Work
- [x] Time
- [ ] Money
- [ ] Donations

SCRIPTURE

Psalm 24:1;
Romans 12:6-7

Service Supplies

You'll need Bibles, plastic trash bags, rakes or other gardening tools, paper and pencils, celery, water, and red or blue food coloring. You'll also need to fill an old purse or canvas bag with a few unbreakable items, such as pens and pencils, notepads, and keys.

Get Set to Serve

This project will take several sessions. The first session will be used to "Get Set to Serve." Kids will learn about being good stewards of the earth and of their church building. They will create a service plan by listing ways they can clean up the church building and its grounds.

The second session will be the Super Service Clean-Up Session, where the kids will actually carry out their service plan. You'll take photos or slides of the kids in action!

Finally, kids will use the photos or slides to present environmental tips along with a slide show at a church event service. Those listening should be challenged to be good stewards of the earth and good keepers of the church building. Perhaps they would even like to contribute to a special church improvement project!

Before beginning this service project, be sure to discuss the scope of the project with your pastor or church office workers and custodian. They probably have some terrific ideas for specific ways your class can help. (They may also suggest that you make it an annual event!)

Before class, set the canvas bag that you prepared in a corner of the room.

Before the lesson, soak several stalks of celery in water that has been tinted with red or blue food coloring. The celery will absorb the color of the water.

After all of the children have arrived, invite them to look at the stalks of celery. Ask:

- **What's happening to this celery?**
- **If this colored water were pollution, what would happen to this living plant?**

Say: **When we pollute our earth, we pollute ourselves and every living thing. There are so many pollution problems today—acid rain, air pollution, great gobs of garbage, a hole in the ozone, water pollution. But, fortunately, there are also many ways we can help. Let's start right here with our church community.** Invite a volunteer to read Psalm 24:1. Then ask:

- **Who does the earth belong to?**
- **Knowing that the earth is the Lord's, how should we treat it?**

Spend some time talking with kids about how God has entrusted us with the earth, our place of worship, and everything else he has given us. Discuss how we should treat those special gifts God has entrusted to us to take care of.

Use the following demonstration using the canvas bag to illustrate how we should take care of things that don't belong to us.

Say: **I want to show you something. Who would like to get my bag for me?** Point to the canvas bag you put in the corner. Call on a volunteer to carry it across the room to you. Make sure to thank the child for taking such good care of your belongings. Then have the child return the bag to the corner.

Now choose another volunteer to get the bag for you. This time, as the child is carrying the bag to you, tell him or her to open it, scatter the contents all over, and toss the bag on the floor. Ask:

- **What would you say to someone who treated your bag like that?**
- **How do you like people to treat your belongings?**
- **How do you think God feels when we don't take care of his creation?**

Say: **The earth and all the wonderful things in it belong to God, who made everything. He trusts us with his belongings, and he expects us to take care of them.** Ask:

- **What are some jobs that need to be done in and around our church building?**
- **What are some ways we could help take care of our church building?**

Lead kids in a discussion about ways to care for your church building. Brainstorm what jobs need to be done at the church and on the church grounds every week. Then invite a volunteer to read Romans 12:6-7. Ask:

● **What are some of the talents God gives Christians?**

● **How could we use some of those gifts to take care of our church building?**

Say: **We're going to combine two of these talents by serving the church community and then teaching others about caring for the earth and for our church building. God calls us to be good stewards, and he also calls us to serve by inspiring or teaching others to do the same thing. So let's get started!**

The Project

Part 1: Planning

After you've finished the "Get Set to Serve" activities, you'll be ready for the first part of this project: creating a service plan.

Create a service plan by having kids list what needs to be done at your church, what steps need to be taken to accomplish those tasks, and what you need to do to get ready to serve.

You may be surprised at how thorough and creative kids can be at creating a service plan! Depending on the age of the children and your resources, service ideas might range from the very simple to the quite complex.

Ideas for serving the church may include picking up trash; raking and composting leaves; planting a tree; planting or cleaning out a garden; checking to make sure the church recycles (and starting a recycling program at church, if necessary); checking for lead in the water; checking for radon or asbestos; organizing an energy audit of the building; or a combination of any of these ideas.

Part 2: Serving

Your individual plans will vary, and so will the time it takes to accomplish them, but here are a few things to keep in mind as you serve.

● Chose a project that fits your schedule. But beware—when kids get inspired, you may find that you're changing your schedule to match your kids' enthusiasm!

● Be sure to obtain all the necessary permissions you need before you begin. For example, if you're planting a tree, you'll need to call your local public service company to check for underground pipes and cables.

● Is your project going to take a few hours to complete? If so, you may want to have snacks and drinks available for your crew. Try to match your snack to the project. Some examples might be broccoli and cauliflower "trees" dipped in ranch dressing; edible "rakes" made from breadsticks with a dab of peanut butter on the end to hold straight pretzel "tines"; or "garbage bags"—brown paper sacks filled with raisins, mini-crackers, nuts, and colored chocolate candies. Your kids will eat it up!

● As you work, you may be witnesses to those who pass by that you care for the earth and your church grounds. Ask kids to be prepared to answer questions about what they're doing!

Part 3: Teaching

After you complete your service project, organize your photos or slides so you can present your examples of service to the other church members. This presentation might take any or all of the following forms:

● a presentation to the church congregation after a worship service or event,

● a bulletin board created by your kids detailing your project and displayed in a prominent place,

● an article in the church newsletter or bulletin, or

● a skit or other short drama explaining what your project accomplished. (Younger kids can memorize a line or two, and older kids can read from scripts that they've written.)

Let kids take the lead (with a little guidance from you!) and present their service project in a way that is most meaningful to them. However they present their project, be sure they include suggestions about what other church members can do to be good stewards of the earth and of your church building.

Project Prayer

At the end of the planning session and at the end of the work time, gather the kids together and offer the following prayer. You may also want to use this prayer when you teach the other church members about your project.

Dear God, thank you for the splendor of your creation! Thank you, too, for this great place to worship. Help us to be good stewards of everything you provide. And help this project inspire others to be good stewards, too. In Jesus' name, amen.

The Extra Service Step

Now take it one step further! Lead your crew in the cleanup of a local public site such as a park, stream, river, or lake. Contact the mayor and invite him or her to join in the effort. Have kids lead tours of the recently cleaned-up site. In the tours, ask kids to stress the importance of caring for God's earth! You can also invite the local radio station, television station, or newspaper to cover the clean-up and tour efforts. Be sure to let kids invite friends to help! (Just make sure you have plenty of adult supervision.)

You may also want to contact these organizations:

- Renew America (For environmental success stories accomplished by kids.)
  1400 Sixteenth St. N.W.
  Washington, DC 20036

- America the Beautiful Fund (Free seed packets for planting! Send a SASE.)
  1511 K St. N.W., Ste. 611
  Washington, DC 20005
  (202) 638-1649

- National Arbor Day Foundation (Free seedlings to members.)
  100 Arbor Ave.
  Nebraska City, NE 68410
  (402) 474-5655

- U.S. Environmental Protection Agency (For more environmental information.)
  Office of Environmental Education
  Coordinator of Youth Programs
  Mail Code: 1707
  401 M St. S.W.
  Washington, DC 20460
  (202) 260-8749

Serving Our Community

As kids explore the fourth ring of service, our community, they'll begin to understand that they don't lead isolated lives. There are those nearby who need our help and prayers. Use these service projects to help kids reach out to neighbors in need.

Kids will gather books to donate to a homeless shelter and make bookmarks to tuck inside their gifts.

Share a Book!

RING OF SERVICE

- ☑ God
- ❑ Family/Friends
- ❑ Church Family
- ☑ Community
- ❑ World

STYLE OF SERVICE

- ❑ Prayer
- ❑ Work
- ❑ Time
- ❑ Money
- ☑ Donations

SCRIPTURE

1 Timothy 6:17-18

Hands-On HELP

Bring in a few books yourself so that kids see you modeling a servant spirit. That way, you'll have extras in case someone forgets to bring in a book or you have a visitor in class.

Service Supplies

You'll need Bibles, photocopies of the "Book Bonanza!" handout from page 72, a two-by-seven piece of tagboard or heavy paper for each child, various stickers, markers, ribbon, pens, and clear self-adhesive paper.

Get Set to Serve

A week or more prior to this service project, send home a "Book Bonanza!" handout with each child.

On the day of the project, have kids sit in a circle on the floor. Go around the circle, and let each child describe one book he or she brought.

After each child has told about his or her book, collect the books and place them on a classroom table for all to see. Then ask:

- **What kinds of books do you enjoy reading?**
- **Do you think God is concerned about our enjoyment? Why or why not?**

Say: **The Bible talks about enjoyment.** Have a child read aloud 1 Timothy 6:17. **God cares about our happiness. He even provides us with everything we need to be happy! Think about all the books you have. Think about all the books you can use from the library. You really are rich in books. We have all those wonderful books, including the Bible, for our enjoyment and for learning about God and his world.**

Some people are not as "rich" in books or other things as we are. Some families have nowhere to live and end up sleeping on sidewalks or in places called homeless shelters. Ask:

- **How would you feel if you didn't have a home to live in?**
- **What would you miss if you had to leave your home?**

Say: **We can serve others who have lost their homes. Listen to this next verse to find out what we should do with the wonderful things God has given us.** Have another child read aloud 1 Timothy 6:18. Then ask:

- **What does God want us to do with what he's given us?**
- **What kinds of things can we share with others?**

Say: **We're going to share our books by taking them to a homeless shelter. We'll also make a bookmark to put in each one. Then we can share the message of Jesus' love with others.**

The Project

Give each child a tagboard strip. Have kids use stickers, markers, and ribbon to decorate the strips as bookmarks to include inside the books. Be sure to have kids write, "Jesus loves you!" on the bookmarks. When the bookmarks are completed, cover them with clear self-adhesive paper.

While children are working, brainstorm with them about other ways they could serve people in homeless shelters. Ideas might include donating items such as clothes, food, and toys. They might also visit shelters with their families or church groups and read books to the children or help serve meals.

Project Prayer

Have kids tuck a finished bookmark into each book, then set the books in the center of a prayer circle. Encourage children to silently pray for those who'll be reading the books. After a few moments, say a short prayer asking God to bless your gifts.

Take the books to a homeless shelter. With their parents' permission, children may want to go with you to help deliver the books. If there's not a shelter in your town, you can mail the books to the nearest city shelter.

The Extra Service Step

Collect books from the entire church to be donated to missionaries. Suggest certain types of books, such as educational books for missionary children to use in their schools and Christian books for adults to use as resources.

book bonanza!

Our group would like to share some good books with children living in a homeless shelter. Do you have any Christian children's books or children's books with a positive message that you'd be willing to donate? We'll be making bookmarks to tuck in the books to remind the children that Jesus loves them.

Please send in the books by ________________________________.

Thank You!

book bonanza!

Our group would like to share some good books with children living in a homeless shelter. Do you have any Christian children's books or children's books with a positive message that you'd be willing to donate? We'll be making bookmarks to tuck in the books to remind the children that Jesus loves them.

Please send in the books by ________________________________.

Thank You!

Permission to photocopy this handout from *Hands-On Service Ideas for Children's Ministry* granted for local church use.
Copyright © Group Publishing, Inc., P.O. Box 481, Loveland, CO 80539.

Help kids give recognition to some community servants with small tokens of appreciation.

Soapy Service Sacks

RING OF SERVICE

- ☑ God
- ☐ Family/Friends
- ☐ Church Family
- ☑ Community
- ☐ World

STYLE OF SERVICE

- ☐ Prayer
- ☐ Work
- ☑ Time
- ☐ Money
- ☐ Donations

SCRIPTURE

Matthew 20:26

Service Supplies

You'll need Bibles, Handi Wipes towelettes or a similar product, permanent markers, soap flakes, a measuring cup, a hole punch, and ribbon or yarn. You'll also need photocopies of the "Soapy Servants" and the "Permission, Please!" handouts from pages 76 and 77.

Get Set to Serve

A week or two before this service project, call a nearby fire station, and arrange for a time that your class can deliver their Soapy Service Sacks. You may also want to arrange to take along cookies and punch on your visit. Also before this class session, photocopy and send home with kids the "Permission, Please!" handout.

On the day of the project, gather the kids together. Ask:

- **What is a servant?**
- **What kind of jobs does a servant do?**
- **When was the last time you were a servant?**

Say: **There aren't many servants today. Or are there?** Ask:

- **What jobs do people in our town do to serve others?**

Have kids brainstorm service jobs in your community. If kids need prompting, suggest vocations such as police work, fire prevention, and medical professions. Then say: **Wow! It looks as if we're surrounded by people who help us every day! We see police officers and firefighters serving the people in our town, risking their lives to keep us safe.** Ask:

- **How many of you have ever seen a firefighter at work?**
- **What are some of the tools a firefighter uses?**
- **How can we help the firefighters?**

Kids might answer that people shouldn't play with matches and

Hands-On HELP

You may choose to explain the service project to the firefighter in charge, and ask permission for the children to wash a firetruck using some Soapy Service Sacks during their visit.

that people should use smoke detectors in their homes. Say: **We're going to show some of the servants in our city, the firefighters, just how much we appreciate them. We're going to make some Soapy Service Sacks to take to the fire station.**

The Project

Ask a volunteer to read aloud Matthew 20:26. Then ask:

- **Why does Jesus say that we should serve others as a servant?**
- **Why is it important to show our appreciation to servants around us?**

Say: **Let's start our service project. After each fire, the firefighters have to wash their firetrucks and check all of the equipment to make sure that it's in perfect working order for the next emergency. We can show the firefighters how much we appreciate them by making these Soapy Service Sacks for them.**

Then we'll deliver them and show the firefighters how to use them. When they drop the Soapy Service Sacks in a bucket of water, let them soak, then remove the yarn, they'll have soapy water *and* decorated cloths to scrub the truck with.

Set out permanent markers, soap flakes, a measuring cup, Handi Wipes towelettes, yarn, and Bibles. Give each child a towelette to decorate on one side with the permanent markers. Then have kids lay the towelettes on the table, with the decorated sides down.

Have each child measure one-fourth cup of the soap flakes and pour the flakes onto the middle of the back of the decorated towelette. Then show kids how to gather up the corners of the towelette, and use yarn or ribbon to tie the soap flakes into a bundle.

Then give each child a copy of the "Soapy Servants" handout (p. 76). Have each child use a hole punch to make a hole in the corner of the handout and attach the handout to the bundle with the ribbon or yarn.

Hands-On HELP

Soap flakes such as Ivory Snow are available in the laundry aisle of the grocery store.

Project Prayer

Before leaving for the fire station, ask:

- **How does serving others with our talents go along with what Jesus tells us about serving others?**
- **What are some special ways you can serve others this week?**

Then gather the children together in a prayer circle. Thank the children for using their gifts, time, and talents in service for God. Then invite the children to hold hands, and ask several volunteers to pray for those community servants who risk their lives every day to keep us safe. End with a group "amen."

Hands-On HELP

Make sure to take a camera with you to the fire station. You'll want to "make a memory" of this service project.

The Extra Service Step

Create your own "firefighter art." Using watercolor paints, have kids paint pictures on watercolor paper. Then fill a spray bottle with water, and have kids lightly spray the pictures with water. The paint on the pictures will spread, giving the pictures an appealing watercolor appearance. Kids may wish to give their pictures to the firefighters or to create a bulletin board for the entire congregation to see and enjoy. Along with the firefighter artwork, you can display photographs of your visit to the fire station.

Soapy Servants

This Soapy Service Sack's for you
To say we're glad for all you do.
You always keep us safe from harm
By fighting fires with each alarm.
So here's our soapy, sudsy way
To say we thank you every day!

Directions

Place the Soapy Service Sack in a bucket of water. Let it soak for several minutes; then untie the ribbon, pull out the scrubbing cloth, and scrub, scrub, scrub!

Soapy Servants

This Soapy Service Sack's for you
To say we're glad for all you do.
You always keep us safe from harm
By fighting fires with each alarm.
So here's our soapy, sudsy way
To say we thank you every day!

Directions

Place the Soapy Service Sack in a bucket of water. Let it soak for several minutes; then untie the ribbon, pull out the scrubbing cloth, and scrub, scrub, scrub!

Permission to photocopy this handout from *Hands-On Service Ideas for Children's Ministry* granted for local church use.
Copyright © Group Publishing, Inc., P.O. Box 481, Loveland, CO 80539.

Permission, Please!

My child ________________________ has permission to go to the fire station

at ____________________________ on __________ from ______________.
(address) (date) (time)

_______ I would like to come also.

_______ I would be able to drive __________ children.
(number)

_______ I cannot go this time.

____
(parent's signature)

____
(parent's phone number)

Permission, Please!

My child ________________________ has permission to go to the fire station

at ____________________________ on __________ from ______________.
(address) (date) (time)

_______ I would like to come also.

_______ I would be able to drive __________ children.
(number)

_______ I cannot go this time.

____
(parent's signature)

____
(parent's phone number)

Kids will touch members of their community with books on tape!

RING OF SERVICE

- ☑ God
- ☐ Family/Friends
- ☐ Church Family
- ☑ Community
- ☐ World

STYLE OF SERVICE

- ☐ Prayer
- ☑ Work
- ☑ Time
- ☐ Money
- ☐ Donations

SCRIPTURE

1 Corinthians 12:4-7

Takeout Tapes

Service Supplies

You'll need Bibles, a blindfold, a marker, a large supply of cassette tapes, several cassette recorders (with good microphones), large nine-by-eleven envelopes, and several good children's Bible storybooks and general storybooks. You'll also need an index card for each child.

Get Set to Serve

Before class, write out the words of 1 Corinthians 12:7 on each index card. You'll need one card for each child in class.

As children arrive, have an attractive display of all the different storybooks, and allow kids an opportunity to look through them. Encourage a few children to pick out their favorite books, and then invite everyone to sit in a circle on the floor.

Say: **We almost have a library here today, and I'm sure you're wondering why. Well, I'll tell you soon, but first we're going to read a few stories.**

Ask for volunteers to read parts of their favorite stories. Ask the first volunteer to come sit with you as he or she reads. Once the child is seated in front of you, tie the blindfold around his or her eyes. Ask:

- **What would happen if you couldn't see? How would you enjoy the book?**

Remove the child's blindfold, and let children offer solutions to the problem. Some may know about Braille and will suggest that. Others may say that someone else could read the book to the person. Reinforce each suggestion positively, then say: **There are people who are unable to see, others who haven't yet learned to read, and still others who are able to listen to a story, but can't read the words from the written page. But everyone still loves to hear a story!** Ask:

- **How many of you can read? Who taught you how to read?**

• **How could you serve others who are unable to read?**

Say: **We all have ways we can help others. God has given us all different gifts. Let's find a way to use those gifts to serve our community.**

The Project

Explain that kids will be recording books on tape for the local library or community center. You may even have a local school that might request specific books needed for special students. By providing the service of recorded stories, the students can reach out to their community.

Let children form groups of two or three. Have each group choose a book to record. Give each group a cassette recorder. You may need to form larger groups depending on the amount of cassette recorders you'll be using. Encourage children to decide on a plan for recording their book. They may choose to take turns, allowing each member of the group an equal chance to read. A group with non-readers may wish to allow younger students a chance to do sound effects during the story. One person may want to be in charge of turning the tape recorder on and off.

Make sure that each child has a task to perform. Explain that each group should find a quiet place in the room. If possible, plan to use several rooms of the church for this project. Have an adult leader accompany each group. Tell children to practice reading the book through before recording.

When children have completed the tapes, gather kids together. Set out the large envelopes, and have children help you place the books and tapes together in separate envelopes. Write the names of the stories in large letters on the appropriate envelopes. Include the name of your church and the address.

Once all of the stories are organized, ask:

• **What were some of the different ways you all helped during this project?**

• **How will these tapes help others?**

Ask four volunteers to take turns reading 1 Corinthians 12:4-7. Then give each child one of the prepared index cards with the main verse written on it.

Say: **Even if some of you can't read this verse, you can have it read to you. It reminds us that there is something special from God in each one of us. Others can see Jesus in your life, and you can help others in your own special way. You can serve! That's exciting!**

Hands-On HELP

If your group is primarily made up of nonreaders, you may wish to provide ABC books for this project. If you have older students, choose books that match their reading abilities and preferences.

Project Prayer

Thank children for using their time and talents to work hard on this special project. Spend time in prayer thanking God for the talents of the children. Also ask for his special blessing on each of the tapes, and that children who listen to the stories might discover God's love. Let children take turns praying a short prayer of dedication for the tapes they've made.

The Extra Service Step

Speak with the local librarian about the possibility of setting up a special listening area for the books on tape. Then have an open house to celebrate the addition. Most libraries welcome extra events like this to help encourage children to visit.

Kids will create a cookbook while bringing attention to the hungry in your community with this food drive.

Create-a-Cookbook Food Drive

RING OF SERVICE

- ☑ God
- ☐ Family/Friends
- ☐ Church Family
- ☑ Community
- ☐ World

STYLE OF SERVICE

- ☐ Prayer
- ☐ Work
- ☑ Time
- ☐ Money
- ☑ Donations

SCRIPTURE

John 6:35

Service Supplies

You'll need a Bible, construction paper, staplers, and a slice of bread. You'll also need photocopies of the "My Favorite Recipe" handout from page 84.

Get Set to Serve

This service project will take a little bit of preplanning and approximately four to six weeks to complete. It will work best with a large group of kids, such as all of the children in your Sunday school, children's church, or club program to contribute recipes; and one class to help assemble the cookbooks.

The kids and the members of your congregation will all be working together for a common goal: stocking the local food pantry in order to feed the hungry in your community.

Before beginning the project, make photocopies of the "My Favorite Recipe" handout (p. 84). Distribute the handouts to your kids several weeks before you will need the recipes. Have kids take several handouts each, and encourage children to write their favorite recipes directly on the handouts or have a parent do it for them.

Recommend to kids that they write their recipes neatly and double check the ingredient amounts before turning the recipes in to a designated location in the church. To gather more recipes, you may also wish to place copies of the "My Favorite Recipe" handouts

(p. 84) in your church bulletin for several weeks. You could also have a cookbook cover-design contest in your church.

After the recipe deadline, make photocopies of each recipe. Two recipes will fit on each sheet of 8½x11 paper. You'll want to make enough copies so that each child can have a cookbook. In addition, you'll need copies for members of the congregation.

The Project

Before class begins, be sure you have enough photocopies of all the recipes. Set out the construction paper and staplers on a table. You'll also need the slice of bread.

Gather kids together in a circle on the floor. Ask:

- **What is your favorite thing to eat on a slice of bread?**

Give each child a small piece of the bread to eat. Ask a child to read aloud John 6:35. Ask:

- **How can bread give life?**
- **What kind of life do you think Jesus is talking about?**

Then say: **Jesus told many parables in the Bible using food. He told parables about grapes, seeds, water, and bread.** Ask:

- **Why do you think Jesus told parables centered around food?**
- **In what way is food an important part of our lives?**

Then say: **In many countries, including our own, people go hungry every day. They don't even have a piece of bread to eat. Many children go to school each day with no breakfast because they don't have any food in the house.**

Jesus wants us to take care of others. He wants us to help feed them. Jesus says that he's the bread of life. The kind of bread he's talking about is different from the bread we eat. Just as when we eat bread we're no longer hungry, when we believe in Jesus we're no longer hungry in our souls. Faith in Jesus can fill up our hungry souls with Jesus' love.

Let's help feed the hungry by creating a cookbook to serve others. We could sell our cookbooks and use the money to buy food for others. But, you know, we could save time if we simply charge people food for the cookbooks! We could "sell" each cookbook for three cans of food to give to our local food pantry. And we'll also be showing others our love for Jesus!

Have kids form the following groups to assemble the cookbooks.

- Cool Coverers. Have kids use construction paper folded in half to create the front and back covers of the cookbooks.

You could easily change the scope of this project by making the cookbooks more elaborate. Kids can use computers and graphic art to enhance the cookbooks, then sell them to the congregation as keepsakes. The money from the sales can be used to buy food for the local food bank.

● Awesome Assemblers. Kids will assemble recipes in each category in the cookbook, placing the cover page as the first page of the cookbook. Categories might include appetizers and snacks, soups, breads, meat dishes, and desserts. Show kids how to place colored construction paper between the categories.

● Steady Staplers. Help kids staple the pages of the cookbooks together to form a binding.

After kids have assembled all of the cookbooks, set up a table in a central location in your church. Make posters to advertise the sale of your cookbooks for a price of three cans of food. Have kids staff the table before and after services in the weeks to come.

Collect all of the cans of food and take them as a group to the local food bank. Make sure to also take a copy of your cookbook for the recipients to enjoy!

Project Prayer

Pray a prayer of dedication over the completed cookbooks at the end of the project. This prayer could include petitions for those who are hungry and for those who will be "purchasing" the cookbooks. End with a corporate "amen."

The Extra Service Step

Create your own Make-a-Meal Baskets to raise money to purchase canned food for the food drive. Choose one or more recipes from your cookbook, depending on the number of kids in your group. Have kids each bring in one or two non-perishable ingredients used in the recipes. Assemble baskets or decorated boxes that include the cookbook and ingredients. Then sell the baskets for a reasonable price.

MY FAVORITE RECIPE

Recipe name: ______________________________

Category: ______________________ My name: ______________________

Here's what's in it: ______________ Here's how to make it: ______________

My favorite Bible verse is: ______________________________

MY FAVORITE RECIPE

Recipe name: ______________________________

Category: ______________________ My name: ______________________

Here's what's in it: ______________ Here's how to make it: ______________

My favorite Bible verse is: ______________________________

Permission to photocopy this handout from *Hands-On Service Ideas for Children's Ministry* granted for local church use.
Copyright © Group Publishing, Inc., P.O. Box 481, Loveland, CO 80539.

Working together, kids will create a small quilt to give to a child in a hospital, shelter, or foster home.

Creation Crazy Quilt

RING OF SERVICE

- ☑ God
- ❑ Family/Friends
- ❑ Church Family
- ☑ Community
- ❑ World

STYLE OF SERVICE

- ❑ Prayer
- ☑ Work
- ❑ Time
- ❑ Money
- ☑ Donations

SCRIPTURE

Genesis 1:1-27

Service Supplies

You'll need Bibles, coarse-grade sandpaper (at least one sheet per child); prewashed muslin fabric measuring forty-four to forty-five inches wide by sixty inches long; an equal length of prewashed calico fabric; fiberfill sheet batting; lots of old crayons; paper towels; a dry iron; and a fabric paint pen.

Get Set to Serve

Gather the kids together. Ask:

- **When you were really young, did you have a favorite baby blanket or toy that you carried around with you? Explain.**
- **When you carried or slept with your favorite thing, how did you feel?**

Say: **Lots of kids have a special object that makes them feel safe and secure. In fact, we all like to have something to comfort us when we feel sad or lonely or scared.** Ask:

- **When are times you feel scared or lonely?**
- **Can you think of some kids who might have a reason to feel upset or alone?**

Say: **There are kids right here in our community who are very sick and have to stay in the hospital for a long time. And there are kids who have been separated from their parents and placed in foster homes. And there are children in families that have lost their homes and have to live in shelters. These kids probably need something to comfort them, too, just as you did.**

The Project

Say: **Now I want you to get comfortable and listen to one of my favorite Bible stories.** Read Genesis 1:1-27 aloud, or ask a few volunteers to read the verses for the class. Then ask:

- **How do you think God was able to create such a beautiful world for us?**
- **What is your favorite part of God's creation? Why?**

Say: **One of my favorite parts of creation is the people, especially the people in this room! I think you're all a very special part of God's creation. I also think there are some kids who might not feel as if they're very special, such as the kids we talked about earlier. We're going to make a Creation Crazy Quilt for a child who needs a little comfort.**

Hands-On HELP

Make sure kids don't print any words on their sandpaper. The words will transfer onto the quilt blocks backward.

Bring out the crayons and sandpaper, and have kids gather around a table. Give each child a sheet of sandpaper. Say: **Draw a picture of your favorite part of creation. You might choose sea creatures, or animals, or trees, or people! First, lightly draw your picture with a crayon on the bumpy side of the sandpaper. Then color it in as solidly as you can. Make a big picture that fills the whole piece of sandpaper, and use a lot of crayon so your colors look bright.**

Hands-On HELP

Ask the kids who finish their pictures first to draw any additional sandpaper squares that you might need.

Let kids help plan how the sandpaper squares will be arranged on the muslin, patchwork-quilt style. Leaving borders between the picture squares and on the sides will create a quilt effect. Choose the number of picture squares that best suits the size of your group: three across and three down; three across and four down; or three across and five down. If you have more than fifteen kids, make more than one quilt.

As kids finish coloring, spread out the muslin cloth on a table, and plug in the iron, set to the cotton setting. Be careful where you place the iron, and warn kids that the iron is hot.

When the squares are completely colored, arrange them face up on the muslin. Then turn all the squares face down on the muslin. Cover each square with a paper towel, and iron slowly and firmly over the entire square. The heat will melt the crayon into the muslin, creating a nontoxic, washable picture quilt.

When the iron transfers are finished, turn off the iron and move it to a safe place to cool. Then hold the quilt top up for the children to admire.

Show kids the calico fabric and batting that will be used to complete the quilt, explaining that you or someone else will sew everything together. Or if your kids are old enough and you have time, consider letting kids sew the quilt together themselves, using the simple tie-through method.

Colored yarn and a darning needle are easy for older kids to handle, and they will love the fun, old-fashioned looking quilt that they create. Just have them sew the yarn up and down at the same spot through the layers, then tie the yarn in a knot on the "good" side of the quilt. Have them trim the yarn above each knot, leaving about an inch. They can tie knots at various spots throughout the quilt. Then you can sew the edges together later.

Bring out the fabric paint pen, and invite children to sign their names under their pictures on the quilt. Also give each child his or her original sandpaper picture to take home.

You might want to have kids create a class card that contains a note of encouragement and an invitation to your church. Deliver the quilt to a hospital or an agency in your community that helps children in need.

Project Prayer

Ask everyone to hold onto the quilt top while you pray: **Heavenly Creator, thank you for all the wonders of your creation. Thank you for the things in our lives which comfort us when we feel lonely or scared. Please bless this quilt, and comfort the child who receives it. Help that child know how much you care. In Jesus' name, amen.**

The Extra Service Step

Take kids along when the quilt is delivered. If appropriate, arrange for them to receive a tour of the children's wing of the hospital, a family shelter, or the foster care division of your local department of social services.

Kids will correspond with seniors in your community through WISE Journals. WISE is an acronym for Wisdom Is Sharing Experiences!

WISE Journals

RING OF SERVICE

- ☑ God
- ☐ Family/Friends
- ☐ Church Family
- ☑ Community
- ☐ World

STYLE OF SERVICE

- ☐ Prayer
- ☐ Work
- ☑ Time
- ☐ Money
- ☐ Donations

SCRIPTURE

Proverbs 13:20*a*; Proverbs 19:20

Service Supplies

You'll need a Bible, spiral notebooks, construction paper, crayons or markers, stickers, scissors, pens, double-sided carpet tape, and photocopies of the "Say Cheese!" handout from page 91.

Get Set to Serve

Contact a nursing home, senior center, or seniors at another church; ask them to be journal partners with your kids for a set amount of time. This will require that seniors will write to your kids once per week or will have someone write what they dictate.

A week before launching the WISE journals, make a photocopy of the "Say Cheese!" handout (p. 91) for each child in your class. Send a handout home with each child prior to the project.

When kids arrive, have them form a circle. Invite children to share their photos with the rest of the group. Encourage kids to each tell the class all about the photo: where they were at the time the photo was taken, if it was a special event, who else was there, and what special memories they have of that day.

After each child has explained his or her photo, ask:

- **What new facts have you learned about your friends today?**
- **What have you learned about new experiences from the pictures that were described?**

Say: **Well, we've all learned some new things about each other.** Invite a child to read aloud Proverbs 13:20a. Then ask:

- **What does it mean to be wise?**
- **What do you think it means to walk with the wise?**

Say: **We all can learn from those who are wiser than we are. We can listen to them, and ask questions, and read what they've written. Listen to what else the Bible says about learning from the wise.**

Invite a volunteer to read Proverbs 19:20. Then ask:

• **Do you think you've gotten wiser as you've gotten older? Give me an example of something that you used to think or do when you were a little kid. How has your thinking changed?** Allow time for each child to share an example. Then ask:

• **Do you think you will get even wiser as you grow older? Why?**

Say: **The Bible says that we should listen to advice and instruction so that we'll become wiser.** Ask:

• **Who do you think has wisdom to share?** Kids' answers might include parents, teachers, older siblings, grandparents, or senior citizens.

Say: **There are lots of people right here in our community who have wisdom to share.** Ask:

• **What was it like sharing your photos with each other?**

• **What would it have been like to bring your photo to class but have no one to show it to?**

Say: **Imagine that you're in a place without your family and that you have some really interesting thoughts to share, but no one to share them with. Sometimes that's what it feels like for older folks in our community. But senior citizens are blessed with wisdom and experience. They want to feel connected, and we need to hear the wisdom of their years. That's where our service project comes in! Ready, get set, serve!**

The Project

For a predetermined number of weeks, children and seniors will communicate through alternating journal entries in the same notebook. The notebooks will be picked up and dropped off weekly so children and seniors can share experiences, advice, wisdom, and faith. Photographs and other small mementos can be taped in the journals.

Set out the spiral notebooks, carpet tape, markers or crayons, scissors, and construction paper. Have kids cut construction paper to fit the covers of the spiral notebooks. Then show kids how to use carpet tape to stick the paper to the covers.

Encourage children to use markers and crayons to decorate the covers of their WISE Journals. Older kids may want to print "WISE Journal" on the covers.

Brainstorm with kids about what their first journal entries should say. Ideas might include information about each child, such as age, grade, hobbies, a description of their family and church, and

Be sure to have each child and each senior print their names on the cover of their journal.

some wishes and dreams. At the end of each entry, encourage the kids to each ask a few questions of the senior partner. This is always a great icebreaker!

Use the rest of the session to write (or for younger children, draw) the first entry. The photographs that the kids brought to class can be taped on the first page or inside front cover of their journals.

You may chose to keep the journals going for a few weeks or even longer! At the end of the project, set up a time for the seniors and children to meet. This can be a simple trip to the senior center to meet their pen pals, or it can be a picnic or party. Some of the children may decide to keep writing to their new friends long after the lesson is finished!

Hands-On HELP

If you have non-writers in your group, be sure to jot down a note of explanation to accompany the pictures. You might want to have the kids dictate what they'd like to say, then add a little note of your own.

Project Prayer

After the journals are finished, gather the kids in a circle. Tell them that they're beginning a marvelous adventure! Not only are they serving seniors in the community, but they'll be hearing some wonderful stories and advice, as well as getting to know some terrifically "wise" people.

Close your time together with a prayer similar to the following. Pray: **Dear God, you have blessed us with so much! Thank you for letting us serve you by serving others. Enrich our lives and touch the lives of our WISE Journal partners. Help us all to learn from each other and to grow wise in knowing you. Guide our writing to be a reflection of the love you have shown to us! In Jesus' name, amen.**

The Extra Service Step

Get the whole church involved! Ask the local senior center or nursing home if there are any projects that need young helping hands. Or how about a game night with kids and seniors? Or cookie crafting? The possibilities—and connections—are endless!

"Say Cheese!"

Next week, we'll be launching a new community service project. Please bring in a photograph of yourself doing something fun! It can be of you on vacation, during a holiday, or just hanging out. (The photo will not be returned.)

Thank You!

"Say Cheese!"

Next week, we'll be launching a new community service project. Please bring in a photograph of yourself doing something fun! It can be of you on vacation, during a holiday, or just hanging out. (The photo will not be returned.)

Thank You!

Kids will create neat little packets of fun for other kids who are going through difficult times.

RING OF SERVICE

- ☑ God
- ☐ Family/Friends
- ☐ Church Family
- ☑ Community
- ☐ World

STYLE OF SERVICE

- ☐ Prayer
- ☐ Work
- ☐ Time
- ☐ Money
- ☑ Donations

SCRIPTURE

Matthew 19:19; Luke 10:29-37

"We Care!" Kits for Kids

Service Supplies

You'll need Bibles, manila envelopes, scissors, glue sticks, crayons or markers, construction paper, and photocopies of the "Care Kit Requests" handout from page 95 and the "Smile Awhile!" handout from page 96. Children will be asked to bring miscellaneous small items to fill envelopes, such as treats, toys, or games.

Get Set to Serve

First call your local food bank, homeless shelter, safe house, pediatric hospital, Red Cross chapter, or police and fire victims assistance programs. Ask if you can donate some packets of goodies to be given to kids who could use a little cheering up. Don't be surprised if they say yes and ask for more!

A week or two before this service project, hand out the "Smile Awhile!" fliers (p. 96) asking for donations of small items suitable for either boys or girls, such as Bible coloring books, crayons, small stuffed animals, books, and small games.

Hands-On HELP

If the packet is for preschool-age children; be sure that all the items inside are larger than a fifty-cent piece to avoid choking hazards. Also avoid items with small parts.

On the day of the project, ask kids to put their donations on a specified table as they enter the room. Children who arrive early can start to divide the donations into categories such as toys, games, and books.

When everyone has arrived, gather kids together in a circle. Ask:

• **What's the scariest or hardest thing that has ever happened to you or your family?**

• **When this happened to you, what did people do to help?**

Say: **Today we're going to find out how we should treat other people who are going through scary or difficult times and**

exactly who we should help.

Ask a child to read aloud Matthew 19:19. Then ask:

- **How does Jesus say we should treat our neighbors?**
- **What does that mean to you?**
- **What exactly does the word "neighbor" mean? Are neighbors just the people who live next door? Explain.**

Say: **Someone asked Jesus that very same question: "Who is my neighbor?" Let's look at a story that Jesus tells to explain his answer.** Have kids take turns reading Luke 10:29-37, the story of the Good Samaritan.

Explain to kids that the Samaritans were the hated neighbors of the Jewish people. To help children understand the significance of the Samaritan's actions, suggest to children that they act out the story. Instead of people, however, try animal characters!

Ask kids to think of two animals that are natural enemies. Ideas might include a cat and a mouse, a cat and a dog, or a fox and a sheep. Have them choose one pair of animals to use, for example the cat and mouse.

Ask for seven volunteers. The characters are the mouse who is traveling and gets hurt, two robber mice, the mouse pastor who passes by, the important church mouse who passes by, the cat who helps, and the innkeeper mouse. With younger kids you may want to act out the story several times to let a new set of kids play the various characters. For older kids, add more passersby.

Say: **At the end of the story, Jesus says that the Samaritan—the cat in our play—turned out to be the good neighbor, although that's not what you would have expected! Jesus says that we should go and behave in the same way, being a good neighbor to everyone we encounter who needs our help.**

So now that we know who our neighbor is (anyone we see who needs help), and how we are to treat them (the way we would like to be treated), we need to discover the best ways to help our neighbors.

Today we'll do just that. We're going to put together special care packets to help kids who may be experiencing difficult times. We'll also share the good news about Jesus—the real way to be able to make it through tough times!

The Project

Set out the envelopes, glue sticks, markers or crayons, scissors, and construction paper. Invite kids to decorate the envelopes with cut-out flowers, smiles, happy faces, or whatever they think would cheer up a child in need. They can also print, "WE CARE! KIT" on the envelopes.

After the envelopes are decorated, have kids each make a construction paper card to go inside the envelope. They may use the messages from the "Smile Awhile!" handout (p. 96), or they can brainstorm a simple, kind message to print inside.

When the cards and envelopes are finished, show kids how to fill the packet with one item from each of the piles of goodies. For example, each envelope might contain one book, one toy, and one game. Be sure to label the outside of the envelope with an age range of kids who would enjoy the packet.

Travel in teams or as a group to deliver the kits, if possible. It's great for kids to actually make contact with the organizations they're serving, and it's an excellent ministry outreach for your church.

Project Prayer

After the "We Care!" Kits are made, gather the kids together, and remind them of the important service they have just performed. Remind them that a lot of children are going to feel a little bit better because of their generosity. Then close with this prayer:

Dear God, thank you for caring about us so much! Because you care...
you give us everything we need to live,
you help us through hard times,
you help us care for others,
and you even sent your Son to die for us!
Help these kits show that we care because you first cared for us! In Jesus' name, amen.

The Extra Service Step

Make this service project an ongoing ministry. Talk with local grocery and discount stores about donating discontinued items or giving your group a discount price on bulk purchases. Team up with another church to put together and deliver the kits to local agencies.

Care Kit Requests

We're going to be making **"We Care! Kits"** for kids who may be experiencing difficult times. These kits will be filled with treats and fun things to do to help kids in need. Please help by donating items to put in the kits.

It would be most helpful if you donate items that are appropriate for either a boy or a girl, such as small toys, games, small stuffed animals, kids' Bibles, Bible coloring books, and crayons. The items must be small enough to fit in a nine-by-twelve manila envelope, but not so small as to pose a choking hazard.

Please bring your donations to ________________________________

by ________________________________.
(date)

We'll make as many kits as we have donations! **Thank You!**

Care Kit Requests

We're going to be making **"We Care! Kits"** for kids who may be experiencing difficult times. These kits will be filled with treats and fun things to do to help kids in need. Please help by donating items to put in the kits.

It would be most helpful if you donate items that are appropriate for either a boy or a girl, such as small toys, games, small stuffed animals, kids' Bibles, Bible coloring books, and crayons. The items must be small enough to fit in a nine-by-twelve manila envelope, but not so small as to pose a choking hazard.

Please bring your donations to ________________________________

by ________________________________.
(date)

We'll make as many kits as we have donations! **Thank You!**

Hard times last for just a while.
We hope this kit will help you smile!

We care!

Your friend,

____
(name)

____
(church)

Jesus said, "Come to me, all you who are weary and burdened, and I will give you rest"
(Matthew 11:28).

Hard times last for just a while.
We hope this kit will help you smile!

We care!

Your friend,

____
(name)

____
(church)

Jesus said, "Come to me, all you who are weary and burdened, and I will give you rest"
(Matthew 11:28).

Permission to photocopy this handout from *Hands-On Service Ideas for Children's Ministry* granted for local church use.
Copyright © Group Publishing, Inc., P.O. Box 481, Loveland, CO 80539.

Serving Our World

With today's media coverage, kids already know that they live in a "worldwide" community. But they may feel frustration at not knowing how to bring about change in the world. Let the service projects in this chapter help your kids serve God by reaching out to children around the world.

Collect pennies from family members, friends, and neighbors to help feed hungry children throughout the world.

Penny Party

RING OF SERVICE

- ☑ God
- ❑ Family/Friends
- ❑ Church Family
- ❑ Community
- ☑ World

STYLE OF SERVICE

- ❑ Prayer
- ❑ Work
- ❑ Time
- ☑ Money
- ❑ Donations

SCRIPTURE

Mark 12:41-44;
2 Corinthians 9:7

Make sure to have some extra pennies on hand in case a child forgets to bring in pennies, or you have a visitor in class.

Service Supplies

You'll need Bibles, pennies, a big soup pot, penny wrappers, tape, and photocopies of the "Pennies, Please!" handout from page 100. Also provide penny-shaped snacks such as sliced carrots with dip, mini-sized round crackers or cookies, and juice.

Get Set to Serve

A week or more before the Penny Party, photocopy and send home with kids the "Pennies, Please!" handout. The handout requests that kids collect and bring in pennies. The event could also be announced in church, included in the church bulletin, and advertised on posters.

Before class, hide pennies around the room for a penny-hunt activity. You'll need to hide about ten pennies for each child. After children arrive, gather them together in a circle. Put the soup pot in the center of the circle. Go around the circle, and let each child deposit into the pot the pennies he or she collected.

Then give each child a few more pennies. Ask:

- **If this were all the money you had in the world, what would you do with it?**

Say: **In the Bible, there's a story about a woman who had only a few cents. Listen as we find out what she did with her money.**

Have children take turns reading aloud the verses in Mark 12:41-44. After the story, ask:

- **Who does Jesus say gave more money? Why?**
- **Why do you think Jesus wants us to share?**

Say: **We know that Jesus wants us to share what we have. The Bible says that he also wants us to have generous, giving hearts.** Have a child read 2 Corinthians 9:7 aloud. Than ask:

- **How does Jesus want us to feel as we give?**
- **How do you feel when you do something nice for someone?**

Say: **Jesus is pleased with any gift we give him—no matter how big or small—if we give it with a cheerful heart. One way we can serve Jesus is by giving to others who are needy. There are children just like you in other parts of the world who don't have good food to eat.** Ask:

- **Think of a time when you were really hungry. How long did you have to wait until you could eat?**
- **What would it be like if you only had these few pennies to buy food for your whole family?**

Say: **You've brought your pennies to share today to serve other children in the world. Today at our Penny Party, we'll play some games, learn more about giving to others, and prepare our penny gifts.**

The Project

Have children play one or more of the following games to celebrate the Penny Party.

- **Penny Hunt.** Give kids three minutes to find the pennies you hid before class. Have kids drop each penny they find into the soup pot before hunting for more pennies.
- **Who's Got the Penny?** Have children sit in a circle with one child in the middle. Have the child in the middle close his or her eyes for a few seconds while you give another child a penny. Then have all the children pretend to pass a penny around the circle. Have the child in the middle guess who has the penny.
- **Year of the Penny.** Have children sit in groups of four. Dump out a bunch of pennies for each group. Children may look at the dates on the pennies to find: the oldest penny, the newest penny, pennies with their birth years on them, pennies from four different decades, ten pennies with dates in consecutive order, and so forth. Give them a time limit and let them share their results when they're done.

When game time is over, have children sit at tables. Dump out a portion of the pennies at each table, and hand out penny wrappers and tape. The children can count out groups of fifty pennies and stack them in the wrappers. If you have a group of younger children, invite some older helpers to assist with this part of the project.

As kids work, discuss what life might be like for the children you'll be sending the money to. Discuss their countries, customs, and culture with your kids. After the pennies are wrapped, have kids wash their hands. Then invite kids to enjoy the "penny snacks" and juice.

Hands-On HELP

If you have access to a variety of foreign coins, bring them in to show your group. The older children may enjoy guessing what country each coin is from. The younger children can make coin rubbings by placing coins under pieces of paper and coloring over them. You could also find out specific information about your church's missionaries in those countries, and pray for them in your group.

Hands-On HELP

You might want to use the Resource Index at the back of the book to choose where to send your donations. Or consider crediting the cash amount to a missionary's bank account.

Project Prayer

Place the penny rolls into the soup pot, and gather kids together in a prayer circle. Have children count the number of wrapped penny rolls, then discuss how this money might help needy children. Have children join hands and offer prayers for those in need around the world. Then close by asking God to bless your kids' efforts and to help the needy children the money will serve.

The Extra Service Step

Consider giving children a "penny goal" to reach in a month's time. (This could be five thousand pennies to represent the story of the feeding of the five thousand.) Challenge kids to collect pennies from neighbors, friends, family, and church members (with their parents' knowledge and approval). Many people have stashes of pennies they're willing to part with. It's surprising how much can be gained from so little, one penny at a time!

Pennies, Please!

You're invited to a Penny Party to help feed hungry children around the world. We'll play games, eat snacks, and have a big penny "wrap-up." Please come!

Start collecting pennies now from family, friends, and neighbors.

When:

Where:

What to bring:

Pennies!

Kids will have a great time cheering on your church-sponsored missionaries!

Rah-Rah, Sis-Boom-Bah!

RING OF SERVICE

- ☑ God
- ☐ Family/Friends
- ☐ Church Family
- ☐ Community
- ☑ World

STYLE OF SERVICE

- ☐ Prayer
- ☐ Work
- ☑ Time
- ☐ Money
- ☐ Donations

SCRIPTURE

Philippians 4:14-17

Service Supplies

You'll need Bibles, a map of the world or a globe, a cassette recorder, blank cassette tapes, a Polaroid camera and film, several colors of crepe paper cut into ten-inch lengths, scissors, tape, paper, and markers or pens. You'll also need a list of your church-supported missionaries and their current mailing addresses. You may want to call each mission to request a specific mailing address for packages.

Get Set to Serve

Gather children together around the globe or near the world map. Spin the globe or point to different places on the map. Ask:

- **Do any of you know people who live in different parts of the world? Who are they?**

Allow children time to share. Then ask:

- **Does anyone know what someone is called who goes away to tell others about Jesus?**

Say: **That's right. A missionary is someone who goes somewhere in the world to tell others about Jesus. Sometimes missionaries travel far away from their families and friends.** Name the missionaries supported by your church, and point to their mission locations on the map or globe.

Say: **Paul was a missionary during Bible times. He wrote letters to people he knew to help them understand more about Jesus. The book of Philippians is a letter to the Christians who lived in the city of Philippi. Let's read a few verses to hear what Paul had to say about some help the people gave him.**

Have several children take turns reading aloud Philippians 4:14-17.

Ask:

- **What did Paul say the Philippians did for him?**
- **And what did Paul say would come to them for the help they offered him?**

Say: **That's right. When we do good for others, good comes right back to us. Have you ever felt happy after you helped someone? That's God's way of blessing you when you do good. Missionaries need help just like everyone else. They need someone to send them help, just as Paul needed help from the Philippians.**

The Project

Have children gather in a close circle around the cassette recorder. Place the blank cassette tape in the recorder, but don't begin recording. Say: **We can't go visit each of our missionaries, but we can send a little of ourselves to each of them. We're going to record our "help" and send it out!**

Ask children to suggest what to include on the tape. One possibility is a team cheer of encouragement. Have children practice one of these cheers: "Two bits, four bits, six bits, a dollar! All for Jesus, stand up and holler! Yea, Jesus!" or "Two, four, six, eight! Who do we appreciate? Yea, (missionaries' names)!"

After the cheer, include a few songs sung by the group. (Let kids pick out their favorites, and they'll sing louder.) Then allow each child to read a favorite Bible verse or offer a greeting.

Have kids make a cassette tape for each of your missionary families. Once the tapes are complete, set out materials to make a pompom to go with each of the mailings. Let children select ten strips of colorful crepe paper for each pompom. Show children how to bundle the strips together and tape tightly around the middle of the strips to form the pompom.

As children work, discuss mission work with the kids. Ask them to consider what missionaries might miss most from home or what kind of food a missionary might eat for dinner. As kids complete the pompoms, ask them to stand together in a group while you take a picture of them. Take one picture for each mailing. Let kids pose as if cheering.

Project Prayer

Gather children in a circle, and thank them for using their time and talents to help others. Ask volunteers to pray for your missionaries during your closing prayer. Close the prayer by thanking God for the children's serving spirits.

The Extra Service Step

Don't stop with one mailing! Remember how Paul mentioned several gifts that he received from the church at Philippi. Just think what your mailings will mean to the missionaries who receive them. Consider starting a pen-pal program with the kids partnered with certain missionaries. It's a great way to encourage current missionaries and potential missionaries as well!

After a guest speaker talks to kids about what life is like for children in another country, the kids themselves will offer a prayer for the children who live in that country.

RING OF SERVICE

- ☑ God
- ☐ Family/Friends
- ☐ Church Family
- ☐ Community
- ☑ World

STYLE OF SERVICE

- ☑ Prayer
- ☐ Work
- ☐ Time
- ☐ Money
- ☐ Donations

SCRIPTURE

Acts 21:1-6

Faraway Prayers

Service Supplies

You'll need a Bible, a map of Paul's travels (often found in the back of Bibles), pencils, and photocopies of the "Prayer for Children Far Away" handout from page 106.

Get Set to Serve

Arrange for a guest speaker to come and talk to your kids. The speaker should be someone who has done service or missionary work in another country, preferably a country with a culture quite different from our own.

If you can't locate such a person, find someone who has traveled to another country on vacation or business. Explain that you want the kids to learn what life is like in that country, especially for the children who live there. Encourage the speaker to bring along photographs or artifacts from the country.

Before class, make a copy of the "Prayer for Children Far Away" handout for your speaker and for each child. On each handout, fill in the country your speaker will discuss. Consider serving a snack that is traditionally served in that country.

Gather the children together and say: **Today we welcome a special guest.**

Introduce the guest speaker, telling the kids that in just a few moments the speaker will share some interesting information with them. Then ask:

- **How does news travel in our country today?**
- **How did the news of Jesus spread throughout the world?**

Say: **Before he went back to heaven, Jesus instructed his followers to go throughout the world and spread the good news**

that he is the Son of God. This is how the Christian church began. The followers of Jesus who traveled and told the good news were the first missionaries. One of those first missionaries was Paul. Paul went to many lands and told the people he met there about Jesus.

If you have been able to locate a map of Paul's travels, show the map to the children. Then explain that parts of the New Testament tell us about Paul's travels. Have a child read aloud Acts 21:1-6. Then say: **This passage is fun for kids to hear because it tells how the children and their parents followed Paul out of the city.** Ask:

- **Why do you think they followed Paul?**
- **Do you think Paul liked meeting children from another land? Why or why not?**

Hands-On HELP

If you have trouble finding a guest speaker, put a note in your church bulletin or newsletter. Most congregations have someone who has lived in or traveled to another country. If not, a church member may be able to put you in touch with someone outside the church who would be happy to come and speak.

The Project

Introduce the guest speaker. After the speaker has finished his or her presentation, encourage the kids to ask questions. Then ask:

- **How are the children's lives in** (name of country) **different from your lives? How are they alike?**
- **Would you like to trade places with the children there? Explain.**

Encourage kids to join you in saying thank you to the guest speaker. (You may want to have the kids write thank you notes to your speaker at another time.)

Project Prayer

Gather the kids into a prayer circle. Give each child a copy of "A Prayer for Children Far Away." Say: **Now that we've learned about the children who live in** (name of country)**, we can understand how their lives are like ours and how they're different. Since we know more about their problems, we're better able to pray for them.**

Ask kids to close their eyes and think for a moment about the children they learned about. Next, ask them to open their eyes and read the prayer along with you.

Then say: **God loves all children. As Christians, we are called to care about children who live next door to us and children who live far away from us. Take your prayer home and hang it in your room. This week, whenever you see it, remember to pray for the children of** (name of country).

Hands-On HELP

Check the Resource Index at the back of the book for names and addresses of a variety of helpful agencies.

The Extra Service Step

Consider having your kids send drawings and letters to children who live in the country they learned about. Perhaps your guest speaker can connect you with a church or school there that would like to receive greetings from your kids. If your guest speaker is unable to help you find a place to mail the greetings, your denominational office or a local mission group may be able to help.

You may want to take photographs of your group to send. Packs of stickers are a great treat to include in a package, along with a cover letter explaining a bit about your group. The cover letter may be in English, even if that isn't the country's native language, since it usually isn't difficult to find an English translator.

Of course, if you receive a reply from the foreign children, your kids may want to continue the correspondence. And consider collecting items to mail to the children, such as crayons, coloring books, stickers, or socks. Your congregation may want to become involved in adding to your collection.

A Prayer for Children Far Away

Dear God,

We pray for the children of ______________. Now that we know more about their country, we can understand what their lives are like. Please take care of them and help them to feel your love. Although their lives are different from ours, we know that inside, they're kids just like us! In Jesus' name, amen.

Kids will create boxes packed with gifts for needy kids around the world.

Shoe-Box Ministry

RING OF SERVICE

- [x] God
- [ ] Family/Friends
- [ ] Church Family
- [ ] Community
- [x] World

STYLE OF SERVICE

- [ ] Prayer
- [ ] Work
- [ ] Time
- [x] Money
- [x] Donations

SCRIPTURE

2 Corinthians 9:12-15

Service Supplies

You'll need Bibles, shoe boxes, and small items for kids (such as hygienic items, school supplies, games, toys, socks, T-shirts, mittens, and hats). You'll also need empty boxes wrapped like presents, construction paper, markers or crayons, Christmas cookies, and photocopies of the "Shoe-Box Ministry Request Form" from page 111. (The request form assumes that you'll be using the charity indicated. Feel free to adapt the form for a charity of your choice.)

Get Set to Serve

This project will take at least two sessions to complete. The first session will be devoted to the "Get Set to Serve" activities and learning about the project. Since items need to be donated for this project, allow plenty of time between the first and second sessions, especially if you plan to use this as a Christmas project.

The next session will be used for packing the boxes and getting them ready to ship. (You may also want to add a few special sessions. One fun activity might be a group shopping trip to purchase gift items with donated money. Another session might encompass the preparation for and presentation of a fun report to the congregation about your service efforts.)

You may choose to use the charity highlighted in this activity, Operation Christmas Child, or another charity of your choice. You may want to contact Samaritan's Purse for current details of the Operation Christmas Child ministry: P.O. Box 3000, Boone, NC 28607, (800) 353-5949. They ship shoe boxes filled with gifts to needy kids in thirty-six countries. These kids are mostly in orphanages in war-torn countries.

Before class, photocopy the "Shoe-Box Ministry Request Form" (p. 111). Also prominently display one or two prettily-wrapped Christmas gift boxes where kids will see them.

As kids arrive, you may want to have Christmas music playing in the background. Form a circle on the floor, then ask:

- **What are some of your family's favorite Christmas traditions?**
- **What do you like to eat at Christmastime?**
- **What was your favorite Christmas present of all time?**

Kids will probably ask who the wrapped presents are for. Just answer noncommittally, or tell kids briefly that the presents aren't for them. Then go on with the lesson. Explain that there are many, many children in the world living in poverty. Ask:

- **Which toy of yours do you think a poor child would love to have?**
- **How would you feel if your family were too poor to buy food for Christmas dinner?**

Say: **Well, lots of kids are too poor to even think about getting presents at Christmas.** Point to the wrapped presents. **Those pretty boxes are empty. I put them there to give you an idea of how poor kids must feel at Christmas, seeing lots of gifts and toys everywhere, but knowing they won't receive any.** Ask:

- **What would it be like if you knew you weren't going to receive any Christmas presents this year?**

Say: **Today we're going to begin a service project to share some of what we have with those kids. But we'll be sharing a lot more than that! Here's what I mean.**

Have kids form small groups of three or four, depending on the size of your class. Give each group a Bible, and have kids in each group take turns reading the verses in 2 Corinthians 9:12-15. Then have kids discuss the following questions in their groups. After each question, invite volunteers to share their insights with the rest of the class. Encourage kids to refer to the Bible passage as they discuss their responses. Ask:

- **How is sharing with others an expression of thanks to God?**
- **How might our generosity affect someone else's faith?**
- **How does the goodness we share come back to us?**

After kids discuss the questions, say: **See? When we give to others, we give more than just the gift, or the money, or the food. We give God's love! And as a result, those people then praise God and pray for us. Let's start giving right now!**

Have kids join you in a circle as you explain the service project. Say: **We're going to ask the people in our church to donate items to fill shoe boxes with helpful and fun things for kids around the world who are too poor to get gifts at Christmas time. Your job is to inspire your family and other church friends to help us by donating items and money. Then you'll help pack the boxes and get them ready to mail. You'll be serving God by serving others!**

Brainstorm with kids what items they think needy children might enjoy receiving and who they might ask to donate to this project. Explain that family, friends, and the kids themselves can donate some of the items, they can donate money to cover shipping costs, or they can do both!

Before kids leave class, give them each a handful of the "Shoe-Box Ministry Request Form" handouts (p. 111) to take with them and distribute. Also make sure kids understand the date when donations are due.

The Project

Session 1: Getting Ready!

You've already done the "Get Set to Serve" activities, and given kids the donation request forms. The "Getting Ready!" session may last several weeks or even months before you plan to pack and send the boxes.

Session 2: Packin' Up!

Set out all of the shoe boxes and donated items. On a separate table set out construction paper and markers or crayons.

Consider having kids form groups with the following jobs.

- Sunny Sorters separate donated items into categorized groups such as books, games, clothes, and hygienic items.
- Perky Packers pack boxes with one item from each category, label the box for a boy or girl, and note the appropriate age group.
- Merry Makers make cards and write notes to be included in the boxes.
- Cheery Checkers check each donated box to make sure it's complete. (Is there a label on the front? Is there a check included to cover shipping costs?)

When kids have finished packing the boxes, you'll need to make sure that each newly-packed box has a check included for shipping costs. Contact Samaritan's Purse at 1-800-353-5949 for shipping details and the collection center nearest you. Or check with a charity of your choice to get shipping information. If possible, have kids accompany you as you deliver or send the boxes off to the charity.

Project Prayer

Gather the kids in a prayer circle. Thank the kids for doing such a great job of sharing God's love with others. During your closing prayer, invite each child to say one thing that he or she is thankful for. And make sure to pray for the recipients of your gifts!

The Extra Service Step

Consider one (or more!) of the following suggestions.

- Team up with another church! Have a friendly competition to see who can collect the most shoe boxes. End the competition by congratulating each other on a job well done!
- Think globally, act locally! Do a thematic drive for local kids during late summer. Collect school supplies and donate them to needy kids in your area. Check with your local schools for suggested supplies and with your local police department, social services department, or food bank for suggestions on how to distribute them.
- Make your Shoe-Box Ministry a year-round event! Collect items to donate all year long and put the boxes together before Christmas.

SHOE-BOX
Ministry Request Form

We're going to be doing an exciting service project with an organization called Samaritan's Purse. We'll be packing shoe boxes with gifts for needy kids in thirty-six countries around the world, many of whom are in orphanages in war-torn countries. The ministry is called Operation Christmas Child. We need your help!

There are three ways to help:

1. Send in a shoe box filled with small items for kids and a $5.00 check. (See "Shoe-Box Explanation" below.)
2. Send in small items for kids and a $5.00 check, and we'll pack the box for you!
3. Send money donations to us. We'll do the shopping and packing.

Shoe-Box Explanation:

Send in a shoe box with small items for kids. You should also enclose a check with each box for $5.00 made out to "Samaritan's Purse" to help with shipping. You may also enclose a card, photos of your family, or a nice note. Please write on the outside of your box if it is for a boy or girl and an age range: 2 years and under, 3 to 5 years, 6 to 8 years, or 9 to 12 years. If you chose the 5-and-under age range, make sure all of your donations are larger than a fifty-cent piece to avoid choking hazards. Put a rubber band around each box, but do not seal them. All boxes will be inspected by Samaritan's Purse before shipping.

Gift suggestions are warm hats and mittens, T-shirts, socks, school supplies, hygienic items, games, toys, books, and puzzles.

Your money donations are due ______________________________.

Your shoe boxes are due ______________________________.

You may bring them to ______________________________.

There are so many children in the world living in poverty. Let's share some of God's blessings with them!

Thank you!

Organize an entire "event" to celebrate the kids' sponsorship of a child in another country. Thailand is used as an example, but any country can be chosen.

Friendly Festival

RING OF SERVICE

- ☑ God
- ❑ Family/Friends
- ❑ Church Family
- ❑ Community
- ☑ World

STYLE OF SERVICE

- ❑ Prayer
- ❑ Work
- ☑ Time
- ☑ Money
- ❑ Donations

SCRIPTURE

Matthew 19:14

Service Supplies

You'll need Bibles, rice, tea, foam paper cups, blankets, several balloons, library books on Thailand, clear self-adhesive paper, pin backs, paper, and photocopies of the "Faraway Friends Festival" handout from page 116. You'll also need photocopies of the picture of the child you will sponsor or pieces of paper cut into two-by-three-inch pieces.

Get Set to Serve

Several months before you want to do this service project, start collecting offerings through Sunday school, children's church, or midweek club donations. The money will go toward sponsoring a child in another country through Compassion International (Compassion International, 3955 Cragwood Drive, P.O. Box 7000, Colorado Springs, CO 80933, 1-800-336-7676). The cost is approximately $288.00 per year.

When the money has been collected, send in your payment and request a child to sponsor. It will take approximately three weeks to receive a response.

Consider applying to your church's missions fund for part of the money needed to sponsor a child from another country. Have the children in your group raise part of the money themselves. Consider employing some or all of the following fund-raising ideas: pledges from each child, bake sales, carwashes, soliciting donations from church members, flower sales, and spaghetti suppers.

When you have received the information about your sponsored child, including a photograph, you can begin planning your Faraway Friends Festival. A week before the festival, photocopy the "Faraway

Hands-On HELP

This sponsorship is an ongoing, long-term service project. Once you begin your sponsorship of this child, you will need to continue in this commitment. Use the fund-raising ideas in this book to keep you on track financially.

Friends Festival" handout (p. 116), and give a copy to each child in your group.

On the day of the festival, gather the kids together and ask:

- **Who has lived in or visited another country? What was that like?**
- **How would your life be different if you lived in another country?**
- **How does God take care of children who live in other countries?**
- **How does God take care of you?**

Say: **Let's open our Bibles to Matthew 19:14.** Have children read the verse aloud together. Then say: **All children are important to Jesus. He loves them and wants them to be taken care of. In some countries, children don't have enough to eat, a place to live, or a school to go to. Jesus wants us to help take care of these children.**

By giving money and donations, we can sponsor a child in Thailand. Our money will be used to buy clothes, school books, and it may even pay for tuition in a Christian school in Thailand. Not only do we need to send our money, we also need to get to know more about this child by writing letters to him or her and by learning about his or her life. Ask:

- **How do you think we can learn more about Thailand?**

Let kids brainstorm ideas for learning about Thailand. They may know someone who has lived there who would be able to bring pictures or slides. Ask for volunteers who will check out books from the library. There may even be a child in your group who has a friend or relative from Thailand. Encourage kids to do their "homework" and come back the following week for the Faraway Friends Festival!

Make sure you photocopy and send home with the kids the invitation for the Faraway Friends Festival from page 116.

Now is the time for you to begin your homework, too. There may be members in your church who have visited Thailand or know of someone who has. Also, check out your local library. A wonderful resource to check out or purchase is the book *Children Just Like Me,* by Barnabas Kindersley, DK Publishing, Inc. This book has pictures and short biographies of children who live in thirty-six countries.

The Project

The day of your Faraway Friends Festival has arrived! You'll need to provide cooked rice and warm tea, enough for each child to

Hands-On HELP

An easy way to keep both the rice and tea hot before children arrive is to serve both from Crock-Pots, keeping the temperature on the low setting. Be sure to keep the pots away from children.

have a small amount of each. As children arrive, have them remove their shoes before entering the room. Greet guests with the *wai,* a common Thai gesture, by placing palms together and slightly bowing the head. Kids may sit on blankets spread out on the floor.

Then serve the rice and tea. Serve both the rice and tea in foam paper cups, encouraging kids to eat the rice with their fingers as the people from northern Thailand do.

As the children are eating, ask what kids discovered about Thailand during the past week. Use this time to share what kids have learned about the country, the customs, the people or the culture. Also use this time to introduce any special guests or any pictures of Thailand. After kids finish eating and sharing information, play the following game.

Say: **Kids in Thailand play a game called *takraw* with a small wicker ball. Let's use this balloon to play our own version of *takraw.*** Have kids spread out around the room, away from tables, chairs, and the rice and tea. Encourage them to keep the balloon in the air, tossing it back and forth from child to child using any body parts except their hands to keep it in the air.

After the game, gather the kids together in a circle on the floor or around a table. Have a child read aloud Matthew 19:14. Say: **Jesus wants the little children to come to him.** Ask:

- **What does it mean to come to Jesus?**
- **How do our lives change after we believe in Jesus?**

Pass out the photocopies of the picture of the child you have chosen to sponsor, or have kids draw a picture of a child in Thailand. If you're using the photograph photocopies, have the kids cut the pictures to about a two-by-three-inch size. Have kids cover the pictures on both sides with clear self-adhesive paper. Glue a pin back on the back of each picture. Remind children that Jesus loves all of the children in the world, and he wants each one of them to come to him.

If you have access to an "instant badge" machine, use it to create more durable buttons.

Say: **Jesus loves the children in Thailand. Almost all of the people in Thailand are Buddhist. Buddhists don't worship Jesus. Many Buddhist children have never even heard about Jesus. The child we're going to sponsor lives with Buddhists all around. Our offering money is helping to pay for him** (or her) **to go to a Christian school where he** (or she) **can learn about Jesus.** Ask:

- **What would it be like to be the only Christian in your family? neighborhood?**
- **How do others know that you're a Christian at your school or in your neighborhood?**
- **Why does Jesus want us to tell others about him?**

Encourage kids to wear their buttons throughout the week to remind them to pray for the child they are sponsoring.

Project Prayer

Gather kids in a prayer circle. Thank the children for bringing their offering money to sponsor the child in Thailand. Let children add additional prayers for your sponsored child or for other children or friends they know who may need to know about Jesus. Before children leave, take a picture of your group to be sent in the next letter to your child.

The Extra Service Step

Cut three-by-five pieces of copier paper. Have kids create colorful pictures to send to their sponsored child. Encourage kids to just draw pictures and sign their names. Do not have them write any additional words on their pictures. (The words would then need to be translated.) If you have many kids participating in this activity, you may need to mail the pictures in two or three of the next letters sent to your sponsored child. The total thickness of the mailing cannot be more than one-eighth inch.

Faraway Friends Festival

You're invited to be a special part of our Faraway Friends Festival.

WHEN: ____

WHERE: ____

PLEASE BRING: Any pictures, friends, foods, books or information you have about Thailand. Contact ____________________ (name) if you have a special guest to bring or will need any equipment (such as a slide projector).

BRING YOUR FAMILY AND FRIENDS! They can learn all about Thailand too!

Faraway Friends Festival

You're invited to be a special part of our Faraway Friends Festival.

WHEN: ____

WHERE: ____

PLEASE BRING: Any pictures, friends, foods, books or information you have about Thailand. Contact ____________________ (name) if you have a special guest to bring or will need any equipment (such as a slide projector).

BRING YOUR FAMILY AND FRIENDS! They can learn all about Thailand too!

Permission to photocopy this handout from *Hands-On Service Ideas for Children's Ministry* granted for local church use.
Copyright © Group Publishing, Inc., P.O. Box 481, Loveland, CO 80539.

Correspond with missionary kids to find out how your class can best pray for them. Then make a missionary bulletin board to remind kids to pray!

Prayer Pals

RING OF SERVICE

- ☑ God
- ❑ Family/Friends
- ❑ Church Family
- ❑ Community
- ☑ World

STYLE OF SERVICE

- ☑ Prayer
- ❑ Work
- ☑ Time
- ❑ Money
- ☑ Donations

SCRIPTURE

2 Thessalonians 3:1

Service Supplies

You'll need a Bible, a camera and a disposable camera, paper, pens or pencils, a world map, and a photocopy of the "We Care! Please Share! Questionnaire" from page 120. Also provide construction paper, scissors, a stapler, and a bulletin board.

Get Set to Serve

Before class, gather information on the missionaries your church sponsors. If your church's missionaries don't have children, contact your church headquarters or a few local churches until you find a missionary family with children about the same age as your students. Then collect as much information as possible about that family.

Gather children in a group and ask:

- **How would you feel if your parents told you that you were moving to a poor country, far away from where you live now?**
- **How would you like it if all your friends now lived hundreds, or maybe thousands, of miles away?**
- **What would you do if there were no malls, movie theaters, or televisions where you moved?**

Say: **Every year kids around the world move to faraway places. They move because their parents become missionaries.** Ask:

- **What do missionaries do?**
- **Does our church sponsor any missionaries? Where do they live?**
- **Would you like to be a missionary? Why or why not?**

Say: **Missionaries are people who travel to faraway places to tell others about Jesus. Our church missionaries live in** (name of country).

Show kids on a world map where the missionaries live. Describe your church's missionaries to the children, giving their names and describing the country where they live. If your missionaries don't have children, go on to describe the missionary family with kids that you located. Then ask:

- **What do you think these missionaries miss most about home?**
- **What do you think we could do for them that they'd really appreciate?**

Say: **Thanks for those suggestions! You know, the Bible tells us about many missionaries. In fact, the Apostle Paul was one of the original missionaries! He traveled to faraway places to spread the good news about Jesus. In the book of 2 Thessalonians, Paul asks for something that I'm sure every missionary would like. Let's see what that is.**

Open your Bible to 2 Thessalonians 3:1, and have a child read the verse aloud. Ask:

- **What did Paul ask for?**
- **Why do missionaries need people to pray for them?**
- **If you were far away from home, would it help you to know that people were praying for you? Explain.**

Say: **This verse tells us to pray for those people who spread the message of the Lord.** Ask:

- **What kinds of things do you think we can pray about for these missionary kids?**

Say: **We're going to be "pen and camera pals" with these missionary children. We can serve these kids by praying for them. But it will help us to pray if we can learn more about what life is like for them.**

The Project

Distribute pens or pencils, and have kids write letters to the missionary children. Encourage children to include details about themselves and your church in their letters. As kids write about themselves, they might describe their families, their schools, sports they like, and hobbies they enjoy. As they describe their church, they might share things they've learned about God or offer favorite Bible verses.

Explain that along with the letters, you'll include a questionnaire to the missionary children to find out how your class can pray for them. Use the "We Care! Please Share! Questionnaire" (p. 120), or develop a questionnaire of your own.

Finally, take a group picture of the children in your class to include in your missionary packet.

Send a disposable camera along with students' letters and the group picture. Ask the missionary children to take pictures of themselves and their surroundings. Suggest that the missionaries send the camera back to you to be developed. Explain that your class will be displaying the pictures on a bulletin board as reminders to continue in prayer for them.

When the missionary children respond, let your class create a bulletin board with the pictures and information received. You may want to consider hanging the bulletin board in a prominent place in the church so the congregation can join in praying, too!

Hands-On HELP

You may want to have kids bring in simple gifts such as trading cards, bracelets, or kids' magazines to send to the missionary children.

Project Prayer

Gather kids in a circle. Ask God to bless the missionary children and to keep them safe and healthy. Thank God for making them willing to serve him.

Then spend class time in prayer for your missionary children on a regular basis. After kids have created the bulletin board, consider using the board as a focal point and gathering place for prayer. Your kids' prayers can be much more specific and heartfelt as they view the pictures and letters they've received. Make sure to mention and pray for any specific requests or concerns the missionary children communicate.

The Extra Service Step

This project will naturally lead to a more permanent writing relationship between your class and the missionary kids. Your students could take turns exchanging letters and pictures with the missionary children. The bulletin board could also be made a permanent project to keep the whole church informed about their missionaries.

We Care! Please Share! Questionnaire

We'd like to learn all about you and your life, and we'd like to pray for you. Please fill out this questionnaire to help us get to know you and your prayer needs better.

- Where do you live? ____________________
- What is the weather like? ____________________
- What is your house like? ____________________
- Who are your friends there? ____________________
- What kinds of unique wildlife live near you? ____________________
- What things do you like about where you live? ____________________
- What things don't you like about where you live? ____________________
- Do you have a television? ____________________
- What do you do for fun? ____________________
- Where do you go to school? ____________________
- How do you get news from your hometown? ____________________
- What kinds of food do you eat? ____________________
- How long have you lived there? ____________________
- What languages do you speak? ____________________
- What is the music like there? ____________________
- What things can we pray about for you? ____________________

Scripture Index

Resource Index

For free seed packets for planting, send a SASE to:
America the Beautiful Fund
1511 K St. N.W.
Ste. 611
Washington, DC 20005
(202) 638-1649

To work with Christians who are united against poverty and hunger, contact:
Bread for the World
1100 Wayne Ave.
Ste. 1000
Silver Spring, MD 20910
(301) 608-2400

To sponsor needy children, contact:
Compassion International
3955 Cragwood Dr.
P.O. Box 7000
Colorado Springs, CO 80933
(800) 336-7676

For membership information and free seedlings, contact:
National Arbor Day Foundation
100 Arbor Ave.
Nebraska City, NE 68410
(402) 474-5655

For information about projects that kids can be involved in, contact:
National Committee for World Food Day
2175 K St. N.W.
Washington, DC 20437
(202) 653-2404

To help needy children, contact:
"Operation Christmas Child"
Samaritan's Purse
P.O. Box 3000
Boone, NC 28607
(800) 353-5949

For environmental success stories accomplished by kids, contact:
Renew America
1400 Sixteenth St. N.W.
Washington, DC 20036

U.S. Environmental Protection Agency
Office of Environmental Education
Coordinator of Youth Programs
Mail Code: 1707
401 M St. S.W.
Washington, DC 20460
(202) 260-8749

Group Publishing, Inc.
Attention: Books & Curriculum
P.O. Box 481
Loveland, CO 80539
Fax: (970) 669-1994

Evaluation for *Hands-On Service Ideas for Children's Ministry*

Please help Group Publishing, Inc., continue to provide innovative and useful resources for ministry. Please take a moment to fill out this evaluation and mail or fax it to us. Thanks!

●●●

1. As a whole, this book has been (circle one)

not very helpful — very helpful

1 2 3 4 5 6 7 8 9 10

2. The best things about this book:

3. Ways this book could be improved:

4. Things I will change because of this book:

5. Other books I'd like to see Group publish in the future:

6. Would you be interested in field-testing future Group products and giving us your feedback? If so, please fill in the information below:

Name ____________________

Street Address ____________________

City ____________________ State __________ Zip __________

Phone Number ____________________ Date ____________________

Practical Resources for Your Ministry to Children

Forget-Me-Not Bible Story Activities

Christine Yount

Here's the perfect activity for your preschool class—week after week!

Now finding the perfect activity to keep every class right on target is easy—with **Forget-Me-Not Bible Story Activities!**

Each **Forget-Me-Not** lesson includes...

•7 brand-new activity ideas,

•an "Extra! Extra!" box with fun bonus ideas, and...

•a completely new way to tell the Bible story!

Plus, activities work with any curriculum—and reach *every* kind of learner in your class: verbal, visual, interpersonal, physical, musical, logical, *and* reflective kids!

ISBN 1-55945-633-7

Creative Can-Do Crafts

Lois Keffer

More than 75 all-new craft projects delight even all-thumbs kids—and mostly-thumbs teachers!

Even "noncrafty" teachers love this book!

From simple paper crafts...to zany tie-dye...to edible dirt soufflé, here are enough crafts to keep an elementary class busy for months...and it's easy for teachers.

These crafts are fun to create...fun to carry home...and fun to show to friends! Plus, they encourage your kids' self-confidence and build their Christian faith. Most crafts include Scripture references and Faith Boosters that tie crafts to favorite Bible stories you want your kids to know!

ISBN 1-55945-682-5

Hooray! Let's Pray!

Your children will *want* to pray every day!

You want your kids to pray...and now there's a kid-friendly way to make it happen!

Hooray! Let's Pray! is packed with activities that make prayer part of daily life. Your kids will discover how to pray with others...pray alone...and how to make prayer more than a fold-your-hands-and-bow-your-head time of waiting while someone else talks to God.

These are best-ever ideas from front-line children's workers—specially selected to encourage children from preschool through 5th grade to pray in age-appropriate ways.

BONUS: You'll get practical help explaining why it makes sense for kids to talk to an invisible God!

ISBN 0-7644-2028-3

The Discipline Guide for Children's Ministry

Jody Capehart, Gordon West & Becki West

It's the hardest thing about teaching...until now.

With this book you'll understand and implement classroom management techniques that *work*—and that make teaching fun again!

From a thorough explanation of age-appropriate concerns...to proven strategies for heading off discipline problems *before* they occur...here's a practical book you'll turn to again and again.

For appropriate, kid-tested, educationally sound solutions for discipline dilemmas, rely on **The Discipline Guide for Children's Ministry!**

ISBN 1-55945-686-8